FIND HAPPINESS BY DISCOVERING

## *Who* YOU ARE AND
## *Why* YOU ARE YOU

KERRY GRINKMEYER

Copyright © 2020
Kerry Grinkmeyer
Find Happiness By Discovering
Who You Are And
Why You Are You
All rights reserved.

No part of this publication may be reproduced, distributed, or transmitted in any form or by any means, including photocopying, recording, or other electronic or mechanical methods, without the prior written permission of the publisher, except in the case of brief quotations embodied in critical reviews and certain other non-commercial uses permitted by copyright law.

Kerry Grinkmeyer

Printed in the United States of America
First Printing 2020
First Edition 2020

10 9 8 7 6 5 4 3 2 1

FIND HAPPINESS
BY DISCOVERING
WHO YOU ARE AND
WHY YOU ARE YOU

# Table of Contents

**Introduction** ....................................................................................1
  *Who is Kerry J. Grinkmeyer and Why Is He Who He Is?*
**Part I**........................................................................................... 12
  *My Story*
Chapter One ...................................................................................13
  *The Beast*
Chapter Two ..................................................................................19
  *Kick the Can*
Chapter Three ................................................................................25
  *Life on Patricia Court*
Chapter Four .................................................................................40
  *My Mother Doesn't Love Me*
Chapter Five...................................................................................47
  *Live with Love*
Chapter Six ....................................................................................55
  *Prayer Will Save My Mother*
Chapter Seven ................................................................................60
  *What About Our Agreement with God?*
Chapter Eight ................................................................................71
  *Running Wild*
Chapter Nine .................................................................................76
  *Meeting Grace*
Chapter Ten...................................................................................81
  *Alone at Camp and a Lesson in Humiliation*
Chapter Eleven.............................................................................101
  *A New Beginning with a New Mom*

Chapter Twelve .................................................................... 117
   *Kobe, You're Dumb – Get Used to It*
Chapter Thirteen ................................................................. 121
   *You're not the Meanest Dog in the Park*
Chapter Fourteen................................................................. 124
   *I Am Capable of Evil*
Chapter Fifteen.................................................................... 129
   *Mom Is Having a Baby*
Chapter Sixteen ................................................................... 137
   *Welcome Home – Your Boys, My Son*
Chapter Seventeen ............................................................... 144
   *Who Decides if You're Good Enough?*
Chapter Eighteen................................................................. 148
   *Fear: You Can Have It or You Can Dish It*
Chapter Nineteen ................................................................ 151
   *You Tried to Kill My Baby!*
Chapter Twenty.................................................................... 163
   *I Can Be Loved and I Can Give Love*
Chapter Twenty-One............................................................ 179
   *Young Love is Different Than Parental Love*
**Part II**................................................................................ 186
   *Discover Your You: What's Your Story?*
Chapter Twenty-Two ........................................................... 189
   *Are You Willing to Change?*
Chapter Twenty-Three ......................................................... 194
   *Uncertainty Breeds Opportunity*
Chapter Twenty-Four........................................................... 199
   *Convert Your Roommate into Your Biggest Supporter*

| | |
|---|---|
| Chapter Twenty-Five | 204 |
| *Building My Personal Brand* | |
| Chapter Twenty-Six | 210 |
| *The Power of Being Relentless* | |
| Chapter Twenty-Seven | 212 |
| *My Plan to Achieve My Goal* | |
| Chapter Twenty-Eight | 214 |
| *Bring Order to Your Outer World by Bringing Order to Your Inner World* | |
| Chapter Twenty-Nine | 218 |
| *What's Next?* | |
| Chapter Thirty | 221 |
| *Create a Flexible Plan* | |
| Chapter Thirty-One | 224 |
| *Commit to Change* | |
| **Epilogue** | **227** |

# Introduction

## Who is Kerry J. Grinkmeyer and Why Is He Who He Is?

June 4, 2005 was the first day of my retirement. It's not a retirement date I chose; I would have preferred to work another 10 years. I was forced out of my own business because my franchisor, Ameriprise Financial Advisors, determined that I was a cancer within their ranks and had to be extracted. I had been one of their top five franchisees for the preceding eight years and was held up as a model to the company's ten-thousand advisors. But now I was a liability, a threat to the structure of one of the largest financial planning firms in the U.S.

Their tool of extraction was the Compliance Department. I had never been fond of following rules, was always looking for and implementing a better way. American Express Financial Advisors had an 80% failure rate among new advisors within their first 18 months of employment. The cost of entry wasn't cheap: You needed an insurance license, a securities license, and to have passed the Securities Series 7 exam.

New advisors were put on the phone and required to cold-call four hours a night, five nights a week, and four hours on Saturday afternoon. For this they received a small stipend for the first year. Of those who lasted, the majority went on straight commission – you eat what you kill – and left within the next six months.

Why would a company operate this way? Because in those 18 months, the newbies moved their parents, grandparents, aunts and uncles' investments over to the company and maybe even sold them an insurance policy. The majority of those newly acquired funds stayed with the firm and were assigned to successful, seasoned advisors.

In my seventh year with the firm, our advisor-employment status changed. We had been independent contractors, but the IRS determined we were more like employees and that AMX would have to make us W-2 employees and offer us all the benefits that the rest of their employees received.

AMX did not want to do this, so they instead converted all 10,000 of us into franchisees and sent us a contract to sign. It was two inches thick. I read it and apparently was one of the few who did. The most important part was that up until this agreement, we advisors did not own our clients; they were owned by the firm. Effective with the Franchisees Agreement, we owned our book of business.

I immediately wrote a letter to every AMX advisor in Alabama and Georgia over 55 years of age and offered to purchase their book of business. Over the next two years, I bought seven businesses and became the third largest franchisee out of

10,000. I converted my business from commission-based to fee-for-service and became the highest-paid franchisee in the firm.

I was a celebrity and preached a new way of doing business that threatened the stability of AMX middle management. I openly degraded their business model which produced an 80% failure rate. My reign at the top lasted four-and-a half-years until Compliance put on the squeeze, which forced me to sell my business to my son, daughter, and nephew.

**Discovering Myself**

I spent many hours trying to figure out what happened. Now 61, I rode my lawnmower around my yard asking myself, *Why they did this to me? Why did they force me out of the business I had built during my peak earning years?* I was angry and that anger became my obsession. Some suggested that I see a therapist. That wasn't going to happen. "I'll work through this on my own," I said.

After months of self-examination, I concluded that I had brought this upon myself. As I looked back at the relationships in my life, whether personal or career, I discovered a common pattern. As a professional, I would join a company and learn the business rapidly. Through hard work and dedication, I would rise to the top. I would receive accolades, but they wouldn't be enough. Recognition of my outstanding performance, trips for my wife and me around the world, never satisfied my desire for approval. I needed an Academy Awards ceremony at least once a quarter.

My personal life followed the same pattern. I was an all-county football player, president of my fraternity pledge class, and platoon sergeant in basic training, but I had no friends to carry forward. The only successful long-term relationship I was able to sustain was with my wife of thirty-nine years, and I had tested her loyalty time and time again. I met Nita in my senior year in high school and married her shortly after graduating from college. It is a marriage of mutual love and commitment but not a marriage of "happily ever after." Again and again I challenged her. I was rude, thoughtless, and self-centered. But through it all, she has stuck with me.

I needed to find out why I was the way I was and why I behaved the way I did. What was the source of my disregard for authority and need to be in the spotlight?

At this point I had lived 22,265 days. I read that the average human can remember no more that 50 to 75 days of their lives at any given time, and those days will vary depending on the time and circumstances in their life when they try to recall them. I took out a yellow pad and started remembering. I'd wait a week and do it again and the article was right. I decided to carry it a step further: "What are the *most important* days in my life?"

I listed what you might expect: marriage, the birth of my children, the death of my mother – that one struck a nerve.

"What were the days or events in my life that made me who I am today and had the greatest impact on my life?"

The answer to that would address my real questions. Why do I always fuck things up? Why can't I make and keep friends? Why am I so hard to love? Why am I so competitive and in need of recognition? Why aren't I happy?

I spent the next six months searching my early memories, talking with Dad, my brothers Butch and Rooney, and my surviving aunts and uncles. The result was *Tall Grass,* a memoir of the first 14 years of my life, which included what I believed were the ten most important events of my life:

1. May 3, 1953, the night in the hospital when my mother, near death, wanted to watch me cry. In that moment and for years following, I felt that I had lost the love of my mother.

2. July 17, 1953, the day Dad came to Cincinnati to inform my brothers and I that our mother had died. All our prayers to God were in vain and I lost my relationship with God.

3. October 31, 1953, the third-grade Halloween costume competition when my stepmother dressed me in drag. I came in second and learned what it felt like to be admired and to be a winner.

4. June 2 through June 23, 1954, the weeks at Camp Anokijig wetting the bed every night and the humiliation I faced every morning. I became determined to be good at something in order to save face.

5. September 24, 1956, the day in fifth grade when I stood in front of class and couldn't spell "second." I was laughed at and cried in front of my friends and classmates and I realized I was dumb.

6. September 8, 1959, the day in eighth grade when my Dad convinced me to join the line of boys "selected" for the football team even though I had not been one of them. I realized that just because someone has authority, they aren't always right.

7. September 10, 1959, the day in junior high when I stood down the school bully. I learned that fear is the greatest weapon that you can hold over another person.

8. May 13, 1960, the day my stepmother accused me of attempting to kill her infant child. I learned that just because someone of authority in my life accuses me of evil, that doesn't make me evil.

9. October 31, 1960, the Halloween night when my friends and I terrorized adults into a near heart attack. I learned that having compassion for others is paramount.

10. October 1961, I found a girlfriend and experienced my first non-parental love. I learned that I could discover love on

my own and that I was no longer dependent on my family to fulfill my need for love, respect, and approval.

Those ten days formed my character and set the tempo for how I would react to every situation that confronted me for the rest of my life. Because of those events, I require unconditional love. If it's offered, I will test it. I will not respond in kind until I am satisfied that you won't turn on me and withdraw your love. Even then, I'm not the easiest person to love. I am an overachiever, never encumbered by self-doubt. I have no fear, other than rejection.

I now understand what my mother was saying. She knew she was dying and would never see her boys again. She wanted to grab any thread of us to take with her. I know that now, but I didn't then, and I didn't for a long time. And at some level I understood Grace, my stepmother. I was an unpolished toy she could make shine and I liked to shine. But once she had her own child, she was done with me. I had been rejected twice by two people I had called Mom, people who were supposed to provide unconditional love.

Maybe, I thought, I wasn't worthy of unconditional love.

For most of my life I felt I was slow. I couldn't read, I can't spell, I didn't know my right from my left, and my memory for facts and figures falls short. I have learned to compensate with my creative skills and my use of logic. At 73 I learned that

I have a cognitive learning disability: I'm severely dyslexic. I gained strength knowing that I'm disabled, not dumb.

**Discover Yourself**

It's my hope that you will do this same exercise to discover "Who You Are and Why You Are Who You Are." Knowing the answers will transform your personal relationships and improve your chances of succeeding at whatever you endeavor to achieve. In addition, it will help you find your passion. It's your passion that will lead you to happiness.

I spent forty years as a salesman because I "knew" I wasn't smart enough to be a doctor, lawyer, or engineer and I didn't want to be a fireman, auto mechanic, or plumber. So, I did what my dad did: became a salesman. I never liked being a salesman. It wasn't my passion. Despite my success in sales I became bored, so I painted, pursued photography, and wrote and now I produce YouTube videos. I am discovering my true passions.

I realize now that I should have been a documentary movie producer. Now retired, all I do is produce content. I believe that the only difference between Lebron James and me is the size of our audience. He's been building his audience for 17 years; I started eight months ago. After you discover who you are, why you are, and what you are passionate about, start building your audience if your goal aligns with mine, or take whatever steps are necessary to follow your dream. You are reading this book because you have something to share, something that someone will need and want to know, knowledge to build your following, your tribe, your community. Whatever drives you, take that first step and the second step will reveal itself.

Technology has made this possible, Oprah built her audience through a collaboration with television networks. Media entrepreneurs Gary Vaynerchuk and Casey Neistat built their audiences over YouTube. Look them up, watch their videos, and then ask yourself what makes them any better than you. Why can they make millions of dollars doing what they love and you can't? Then watch my videos and tell me what I've got over you. I can tell you one of those things: On September 23, 1960, I stood up to a bully, Bill Sidney, and told him that the line started behind me.

If you hesitate in taking up my challenge, is it because of fears you took on in your youth that you've been carrying for years? It's time to put them down.

**Book Structure: My Story and then Your Story**

I begin the book In Section 1 with the story of the first fourteen years of my life. You will come to know me as I know myself and it will help you understand how I got there. You'll see that I've freed myself of many burdens and come to better understand those I continue to work on. In many cases, I've turned those burdens into assets. And in reading my story, I hope to inspire you to write your own story and put your life on a path to happiness. This process will help you gain a greater understanding of who you are and why you are who you are – as it did for me. I encourage you to self-publish your story so others can learn from it and because, more importantly, it will serve as the pivot point in finding your passion and finding happiness.

I know little to nothing about my grandfathers and grandmothers and absolutely nothing about my great grandparents and beyond. But I know a lot about George Washington and Abe Lincoln because someone wrote their story. I don't suspect anyone will write *your* story, so you need to write it yourself. At the end of this book, I'll point you in the direction to get this done.

I can guarantee that once you discover who you are, why you are who you are, and the essence of your true passion, you will be compelled to initiate change in your life. This is the hard part. You may need to change your relationships, your job, and your beliefs about your limitations. But change is good. It will take you where you want to go, even if you aren't quite sure where that is.

Section 2 of the book will help guide you in that process. It will focus on how to overcome all the negative self-speak and self-doubt you've acquired in your life up until this time.

You will discover that your limitations are self-imposed and that you have the power to achieve whatever you set your mind to achieve. This will require a new mindset and a new level of commitment, but as a result of your process of self-discovery, you will gain a level of focus that you never had before. The end result: happiness.

It took me 74 years to get to where I am today. I can honestly tell you I have never been happier. I wish this for you.

# Part I

## My Story

# Chapter One
## The Beast

Katherine Agnes Grinkmeyer woke up on May 3, 1953, in a fetal position. She was clean and she wasn't nauseated – it had been a good night. Carefully, she rolled on to her back. The beast had slept as well but was waking; its grip on her left side was firm and unrelenting so most of her effort came from her right. She pushed an extra pillow in place for support and struggled to sit up.

The morning sun poured through her window and lit her private room in Carle Memorial Hospital in Urbana, Illinois, part of the University of Illinois medical school. Her family couldn't afford a private room but the treatments she was receiving required careful observation and isolation. Her husband, Chuck, urged her not to worry about the money. They'd figure that out after she got better and came home.

Everything had changed so quickly. Just seven months earlier, she, Chuck, and their three boys had moved to Champaign from Cincinnati, eager to start a new life. They had hardly settled in when, three months later, she was diagnosed with breast cancer and everything began to fall apart.

"Kay" felt lucky that her home was a leader in cancer research which was then in its infancy. She chose this hospital to try a miracle cure, a treatment first known as Drug X. It had been developed by Dr. Stevan Durovic, a controversial Yugoslavian physician who believed the sperm of thoroughbred horses might help battle malignancy. When his compound was injected into patients in Argentina, it had reportedly stopped cancer in its tracks and regenerated damaged cells. The research so intrigued Dr. Andrew Ivy of the UI medical school that he sought and received approval from the American Medical Association to do limited trials of Krebiozen, as the mysterious drug was eventually called. It sounded crazy, sure, but what did she have to lose? The three months of injections would be free but required her to stay in the hospital the entire time. Only Chuck would be able to visit. She would be separated from her boys, her precious boys.

Now comfortably sitting, Kay reached into the nightstand for her rosary. She stopped and gazed at her hands. These are not the hands of a 29-year-old mother, she thought. They look like they belong to a woman of 80. Four months ago she weighed 132 pounds; now she was 98 pounds of skin and bone. Her skin was pale, even for a red head, and her beautiful hair, her pride, was rapidly thinning.

She adjusted her wedding ring. If she wasn't careful, she'd lose it, her fingers were so thin. *Papa, you gave me this, but what else have you given me?*

Her father had been a barber and a bookie in Saint Bernard, Ohio. The 1.5 carat diamond, a pay-off on a large gambling debt, had become her engagement ring. She hoped that one day it could be passed on to a granddaughter; but now she wondered if she would ever live to see one. When Kay was a teenager, Papa had died of cancer.

Rosary in hand, she started:

*Hail Mary, full of grace,*

*Our Lord is with thee.*

*Blessed art thou among women,*

*and blessed is the fruit of thy womb,*

*Jesus.*

*Holy Mary, Mother of God,*

*pray for us sinners,*

*now and at the hour of our death.*

*Amen.*

*Lord have mercy on me.*

*God have mercy on me.*

Kay was a devout Catholic, but in the last few months her faith had begun to waver. "Why me, Lord?" she had wondered. "I'm a young woman, in a strange place, and I now find myself in Hell. What did I do to deserve this?

*Lord have mercy on me.*

"Jesus, why are you letting this happen to me?"

*God have mercy on me.*

She finished and crossed herself with the crucifix at the end of her rosary,

*In the name of the Father, the Son, and the Holy Ghost.*

*Lord my savior, please forgive me for questioning you.*

She would have to acknowledge her loss of faith next Sunday when the priest from Holy Cross came to the hospital to hear her confession and give holy communion. But this would be a better day, she thought. Chuck is bringing Butch and Kobe (me) to the hospital this evening. She hadn't seen her boys in four months.

Unfortunately, the Krebiozen injections had shown no measurable improvement. In fact, the cancer had spread from her left breast into her armpit and the doctors feared it would soon attack her spine. That's why radiation treatments were added. For Kay, it was a new circle of hell, a new indignity. The doctors had made it sound so simple. "We're going to try a more aggressive treatment, radiation. We have a new 300-MeV betatron. It's a super X-ray machine developed here at the university by our own professor Donald Kerst. The betatron will focus massive amounts of radiation through a particle accelerator. It will kill the cancer in your body and likely stop its spread."

Twice a week she was taken into a cold room and placed on a table. A technician aimed the pointy tip of a large machine at her chest and side. She never asked why everyone left the room when the it started. She didn't want to hear the answer. Instead she focused on the loud *MIRRRR* of what sounded like a monster on the other side of the wall.

It must take a monster to kill a beast, she reasoned.

The next day would bring twelve hours of vomiting, nausea, and diarrhea. Radiation sickness. This had become routine, almost acceptable, as long as it was followed by a peaceful night of sleep. This is when she really began to lose weight because she had trouble swallowing and was constantly tired.

But that wasn't the hardest part. It was the isolation. "You won't survive an infection," she was told, so few visitors were allowed. She hadn't seen her mother since they left Cincinnati. Her only contact had been the Saturday night phone calls. Chuck came by as often as he could, but he had to work his new sales territory and that meant he was out of town three out of four weeks and only home on weekends. Rooney, her baby. was back in Cincinnati with Chuck's mother, while Butch and Kobe were here in Champaign, watched over by housekeepers. It couldn't be good for them. Boys that age need their mother, but they had not been able to visit -- part of the isolation. Where is all the money going to come from? she wondered again.

She clutched her rosary and closed her eyes.

Annie, her day nurse, entered the room at 8:45 a.m. She had cared for Kay for the past four months and had become more of a friend then a nurse.

"This is a big day," she said. "We've got to get you all cleaned up, fattened up, and prettied up. I've brought some rose water for your bath and some make-up."

"Annie, I don't wear make-up."

"Am I your friend?

"Yes, you're my friend."

"Would I steer you wrong?"

"No."

"Then trust me, you need make-up this evening if you don't want to scare the bejesus out of your boys. Plus, we're going to have to work on that hair." Annie spoke with authority. "What do you want for breakfast?"

This is going to be a good day, Kay thought again. It was nice of the doctors to allow us to break the rules and let the boys come to the hospital this evening. I must be getting better.

This will be the start of many good days . . . I hope.

# Chapter Two
## Kick the Can

The Catholic Church describes communion as the moment the Holy Ghost enters the soul of those who have been baptized. To believers it's a sacrament, a moment of religious perfection. And on May 20, 1951, at the age of seven, I committed my life and soul to God, Jesus, and the Virgin Mary.

In that glorious moment as I approached the priest to take my first communion, I felt secure, loved. Part of an extended family of grandparents, aunts, uncles, and cousins. But over the next 26 months, God, Jesus, and the Virgin Mary would forsake me. My mother would scare me and then be taken from me. My father would withdraw from me. And I would leave my extended family. I would learn to depend on my older brother to survive.

It's only now, more than half a century later, that I can look back and realize that my entire life was shaped by events that took place during those formative years. These separate but intertwined shocks would nearly destroy my ability to love and interact with others. They would erode my respect for authority, and ultimately they would create the conditions that could make me a success – or guarantee my failure – in everything I pursued the rest of my days.

I believe that our character forms early in life. What I find unique is that I took the time and effort to figure myself out. This is my story.

~ ~ ~

We moved to Champaign from Cincinnati in the winter of 1952 when I was seven. It was Mom and Dad, my older brother Butch, my baby brother Rooney, and me. We were typical of the time and place: three Catholic boys being raised by an aspiring father and mother who hoped to make a better life for their family.

My parents saw the move as an opportunity to get ahead. We could not live in the house of my mother, Grandma Talon, forever – there were five of us now. It would be hard leaving our friends on Church Street, but Butch and I had each other and Rooney was just two and too young to care. The center of his world was Mom.

My older brother Butch was conceived a few days before Dad joined the Coast Guard in 1942. Chuck had met Kay at a roller rink and had dated for several months before he got his Army draft notice. His buddies had warned him about Army life so he tried to enroll in the Navy or Air Force, but they couldn't take him because he had already been ordered to report to the

Army. Then he stumbled onto the Coast Guard recruiting office at the courthouse. The agency wasn't bound by the same recruitment rules. He joined the Coast Guard on a Friday, proposed to Kay on Saturday, and sought her mother's permission on Sunday. The couple married the following Sunday and Dad boarded a train to Oakland on Wednesday. Butch was born nine months later.

Chuck moved up the ranks quickly to become a sergeant teaching signal school when he sent for his wife and son to join him. He had rented a one-room apartment for $17.50 per month. Chuck ran the school in the afternoon, worked as a longshoreman several nights a week, and slept in the morning. Kay passed her time with Butch and the other military wives. She enjoyed the California weather but missed her mother and hated spending so much time alone while Dad was working. Then Chuck got assigned to a ship, which required spending up to a year at sea. Six months after arriving, Kay returned to Cincinnati with Butch in her arms and me in her belly. I spent the first seven years of my life in Cincinnati.

~ ~ ~

The movers took our furniture two days before our move to Champaign, Illinois. Mom placed blankets and pillows on the floor where their bed once stood, and all five of us slept there together for those last two nights. Butch and I rode on Dad's back like a cowboy on a horse, and I wished desperately that

Mom had not already packed away my Gene Autry toy gun. But I don't remember ever having so much fun as those two nights, rolling and laughing on the bedroom floor. For one of the last times, we were all together.

Although we called him Rooney, my youngest brother was named Jerry. He was born on December 13, 1950, and came home from the hospital just before Christmas. Uncle Eddie had played Santa on Church Street that year, although I was so taken by the costume and beard, I hadn't recognized him. That was the year Gene Autry had a number one hit, *Rudolph the Red-Nosed Reindeer,* and Santa had brought us a copy that we played on the crank-up RCA Victor phonograph. We all decided that baby Jerry's nose was so red that he looked like Rudolph, and that's how he became known as Rooney.

Butch and I were leaving our friends in the Saint Bernard neighborhood but we were looking forward to the adventure in Champaign. As in most families, the center of our life was our Mom. She was always there for us, and her love was abundant and readily accessible. I didn't notice that she wasn't feeling well, and I'm sure she wanted it that way.

Dad had taken a new job with Williamson Heating and Cooling, and his new territory was based in Champaign. Chuck Grinkmeyer had done a lot of things after leaving the service. He had been a blackjack dealer at a casino in Covington, Kentucky. He worked at a slaughterhouse owned by one of his uncles. He was even a press operator at the Beau Brummel Tie Company. Looking back, we were poor, but I had no way of knowing it. Champaign, I see now, was expected to be a real opportunity for us.

Our new home, Number 1 Patricia Court, was the first house of four along one side of what used to be a farmer's path to his hay barn. The barn still stood at the end of the road and would provide Butch and me with many adventures over the coming years. All four houses looked exactly the same only trimmed in different colors – ours was in red. It had three bedrooms, one bath, and a living room and kitchen all tucked into 600 square feet. A gravel driveway pulled up to the back door. There were no trees or shrubs and only weeds for grass. We were surrounded by nicer brick homes with trees and grassy yards and concrete driveways.

We quickly found friends and often played Kick the Can, a variation of "hide and seek" that had to be played after sunset – in the dark. On one evening, Sylvia is "It." She stands in the middle of the street on a clear summer night next to a tin can, shuts her eyes, and counts to 20. The rest of us, aged 7 to 12, run to hide. According to the rules, you cannot hide anywhere that would not be visible if the sun were up. Once a "Hider" is spotted by the person who is It, they both must race back to kick the can. If the person who is "It" kicks the can before the Hider, the Hider becomes It. The person who was It hollers

"Ally-ally in-come free," the other Hiders emerge, and the game starts over.

Sylvia is eleven, has black hair, and is tall for her age. She never smiles much but is always nice. She always wears a dress, never shorts or pants like the other girls. Sometimes she would invite me over to play cards on Saturday.

"Kobe, you can't keep hiding in the same place," she told me a few days earlier while we were playing cards in her front room with the drapes pulled across the windows. "Everyone knows where you like to hide and they can always find you in that ditch."

But there I am again, hiding face-down in the ditch in tall grass next to a drainage culvert. If Sylvia wanders past the Monroe's mailbox in search of another Hider, I will sprint to the can and kick it, sending it spinning high into the darkness. I'm one of the younger players so I don't often get "home free." In fact, I seem to spend a lot of time being It but I like the game anyway. I like being included with the neighborhood kids.

Thinking back now, I can see my childhood was like the can. I was flying through the air in a game I didn't – couldn't – understand. And soon enough, I would crash to the earth.

# Chapter Three
## Life on Patricia Court

Mom had not been feeling well in the summer of 1952. She slept a lot and complained of back pain, which was not like her. Even before we moved, there had been a question of whether she would be able to care for Rooney by herself. In Cincinnati, she had her mother to help her, and it had been a tough decision to leave. Grandma Tallon didn't want us to go but she couldn't keep Rooney because she worked at a hospital. It was suggested that Aunt Ruthie, Dad's youngest sister who still lived at home, could help Grandma Grinkmeyer with Rooney. But Mom would not allow it. "Rooney is coming with us," she declared. "We're a family and we're staying together. I'll manage."

Mom's doctor, Dr. DeCourcy, who had delivered all three of us boys, assured Mom and Dad that the lump in her breast was nothing more than a swollen milk gland. "After all, Kay, you've had three healthy boys," he had assured her. "The lump will go away in several months and you'll be fine."

Mom, who came from strong Irish and German stock, had never been frail. She loved to roller-skate, even continuing after she became a mother. She was five-foot five, weighed 130 pounds, had striking auburn hair, and wore glasses to read. At 27, she was still pretty and proud of her boys.

At first, our life seemed normal on Patricia Court. We spent most the time outside while Mom looked after us. Dad was developing his territory, which covered most of Illinois and some of Indiana, so he wasn't around during the week. He got a small monthly salary and then a commission check once a year, so it was important that he get off to a good start.

On the weekends Dad came home and would play baseball with Butch and me while Rooney sat on the ground next to him. We had no other family in Champaign, so the picnics and get-togethers were no longer a part of our life.

One Friday night Dad brought home a lawnmower that one of his dealers had given him. That meant Saturday would be devoted to cutting the weeds that served as grass.

"Dad, can I cut the grass?" I asked for the fifth time.

"No, you're not big enough to use a power mower," he had answered again and again.

"I'm almost as big as Butch, and you're letting him cut the grass."

I finally wore him down.

"Okay, you can go around once, but only once."

"Okay!" I agreed in victory.

When Butch turned the corner, Dad motioned for him to relinquish the mower. He placed me behind it, positioning my hands on the push bar, which was at eye level. Then he shouted final instructions into my ear. "Just push here and don't take your hand off this bar." And I was off.

I finished the first side of the square I was to cut and made a left turn. I looked over my shoulder toward Dad and Butch, seeking approval. They both waved me on. I was doing great. I finished the second side and made another left turn. But halfway down this side I spotted the can from our game directly in front of me. I stopped short and looked back at Dad for instructions. He waved me on. *Surely not over the can?* I thought.

I dropped my hands from the bar and started to take the can out of my path. This prompted an emphatic "No" from both Dad and Butch that I could hear over the roar of the mower. They both started to move toward me.

*Oh, no you don't*, I thought. *You're not going to get this mower from me. This is my turn.* I jumped back behind the mower and pushed ahead. Dad had waved me on, so I figured that when you find a can in your path, you run right over it. No big deal, I imagined. This was 1952 and it was a sizable tin can. Aluminum cans were not yet in wide use. As I rolled over it, the mower blade hurled the can against the steel housing, creating a noise that I imagined would be similar if one of the planes that flew over our house from the Air Force base crashed to the ground.

The awful grating continued for three interminable seconds until the can flew out of the mower right at Dad and Butch, who were now running toward me. The two of them hit the ground and the can flew over their prone bodies. I pushed on and quickened my pace, not wanting to forfeit my turn until I reached the end of my promised round.

Dad and Butch gathered themselves just in time to meet me at the finish line. "Why the hell did you run over that can?" Dad shouted over the roar of the mower. Butch had his "stupid little brother" look on his face.

The word "hell" scared me a bit. This wasn't acceptable language in our house. "You told me to," I replied with waning confidence that I had done what I was supposed to do.

"You don't run over cans or anything else with a power mower. You should know that."

"That's what I thought, but you and Butch waved me on over it." Tears were forming in my eyes, and Dad saw that there was no point in making me feel worse.

"Yeah, I guess I did wave you on," Dad said, softening a bit. "Don't worry about it. But in the future go around rocks and cans. Okay?"

"Yeah," Butch added like he had been cutting grass his entire life and only a dummy would do such a thing. "You don't run over stuff."

I swallowed hard and uttered weakly, "I'll see if Mom has another can for our game tonight. That one won't work anymore."

I headed to the house, confident that even if Dad was angry, Mom would see it my way and I'd be fine. My mother was the peacemaker in our home. She wanted everybody to be happy and would not allow bickering or fighting. In those early years of my life, Mom was my anchor.

Shortly after, Dad took her to the hospital at the University of Illinois because she wasn't getting better and her doctor couldn't figure out what was wrong. They came home and talked over dinner. That was the first time that I heard the word "cancer." I didn't know what cancer was, but I got the idea it meant that something bad was growing in Mom's body. Butch, Rooney, and I were sent to our room, but we could hear them talking about treatment, money, looking after the boys, and how long Mom would be away.

"What's cancer?" I asked Butch.

"It's something that Mom's got, and she has to go to the doctors to get rid of it, I guess," he said with an edge to his voice, like he was mad at me.

Rooney played on the floor, unaware that his life was about to change forever. Eventually, any memories he had of his mother would fade. She would become someone mentioned briefly in passing conversation. Years later he would swear that she returned to reassure him in the middle of the night as he despaired over a failing business.

I was scared but felt sure Dad would see to it and Mom would make everything all right for everyone. After all, that's what moms and dads do.

My parents called Cincinnati the next day and it was decided that Rooney would return to live with Grandma Grinkmeyer until Mom got better. Butch and I would stay in Champaign. For the next several days Mom wouldn't put Rooney down, afraid, it seemed, that if she did, she would never pick him up again.

I overheard her tell Dad, "If something happens to me, you bring Rooney back to Champaign to grow up with his brothers. Chuck, you promise me you will."

"Kay, nothing is going to happen to you. We'll all be back together again in a matter of weeks. You're going to be okay."

That weekend Dad took Rooney to Cincinnati. My baby brother would never see his mother again.

"Mom, why is Rooney going to live with Grandma Grinkmeyer?" I finally asked.

"I'm not feeling well and I won't be able to take care of him for a while."

"But you'll still be able to take care of us, won't you?"

"Sure I will, but you two are older and can help me around the house while I get better."

"From the cancer?"

"Yeah, from the cancer," she answered with a weary look and her face seemed to age right in front of me. She left the kitchen and went to her bedroom.

Several weeks later, Dad took Mom to the hospital. Dad hired the first of what would be several housekeepers to look after Butch and me while he was on the road or spending time at the hospital.

Mrs. Elkins was typical. She stood about five-foot, three inches tall and weighed over 220 pounds. She didn't bathe – at least not at *our* house – and had a distinctive odor about her, something like sour milk. She was a good cook but not much of a housekeeper. I remember Mrs. Elkins because she stuck around longer than anybody else. I suspect it was because she needed the money.

"Now here are my rules while I'm looking after you," she told Butch and me that first day. "I make dinner at night and sandwiches for lunch; you eat cereal for breakfast. I keep the house clean. You two stay out of the house except to eat and sleep. I go home on Friday night and come back on Monday morning. You get your bath on Saturday when your dad is home. What happens here during the week is between us. I don't bother your dad with what you get into, and you don't bother your dad with what I'm doing. Do you understand?"

"I understand," we both said, more confused than anything else.

And that was how it worked. We left the house in the morning, came by to pick up a sandwich, returned for a sit-down dinner, left the house again, and came back around nine, when we went to our rooms and to bed. On most nights, Mrs. Elkins would be sleeping on the couch or talking on the phone when we came home. On the weekends, Dad went to the hospital and we were again on our own. Butch and I were now eight and nine years old, essentially living on our own.

I really didn't know what was going on; I just knew Mom was sick but figured she was getting better. I think Butch had a better idea of the reality. He was always mad, and it was about this time that he and I started fighting. And not just with words – with fists.

We were still the best of friends, but it seemed that anything I did could irritate him and he'd be more than happy to smash me in the face or pound the breath out of my stomach. It was as if we were starved for any expression of emotion and this was the best we could come up with.

We started to get a reputation in the neighborhood – not one we rejected – and became known as the Grinkmeyer Gang. We settled our differences with our fists. Parents told their kids to come into the house if they saw us coming down the street. We didn't steal anyone's milk money or anything like that, but we were out of control. Dad wasn't around and the housekeepers didn't seem to care, so we continued down that path.

One day a neighbor told us, "You boys are not to come into our yard, and my kids are not to play with you. Don't come back here."

We were out of school on summer vacation and didn't have toys or bikes, so we scavenged wood and nails and built a fort in front of the hay barn at the end of Patricia Court. We caught snakes and mice and cooked them over a fire. I don't remember eating them, but we forced other kids to. I'm sure we would have fed them to Rooney if he had been there. Our days were filled with roaming the neighborhood, playing football in Mike Swartz's backyard, or hiking down the country road.

Robinson Woods was about three miles from our home. It was nothing more than a stand of trees on the edge of a corn field. What made it special was a creek that ran through it, usually after a hard rain. We would walk there and swim when it was flowing. We knew it wasn't clean because you could often see different colors in it. One day Barry Moore, a red-headed boy with freckles, brought a canteen and some water-purification tablets that he got from his older brother in the Boy Scouts. Following the instructions as best we could, we filled the container with creek water, dropped in two small tablets, and waited for about thirty minutes. None of us had a watch so we guessed, all anxious to drink some of our purified water.

"You go first," Butch said to Barry.

Barry took a sip and smiled. "What's it taste like?" I asked.

"Kinda sour, but good. Yeah, it's good."

And so the canteen was passed around for all to enjoy. Refreshed, we went back to swimming in the creek.

As the sun began to set, we gathered our stuff and started the three-mile hike back home. It had been a fine day and we'd had a new adventure. It seemed that each day offered a new adventure. But about a mile into our walk, Butch stopped in mid-step. "I think I'm going to throw up."

We urged him on, assuring him not to worry. We had all brought and shared lunch and figured it couldn't have been anything we had eaten. Soon Butch was in the ditch puking his guts up. This was no big thing – we had all thrown up before – but this was different. Butch couldn't stop. He just kept throwing up even when nothing was left. He lay in the ditch without a shirt, his stomach heaving in and out.

"He's really sick. We better get him some help."

"He's turning white and can't breathe!" The rest of us stood on the road watching. This continued for two more minutes but no one went for help.

As suddenly as he had started, he stopped and laid still. Finally, someone spoke up.

"Butch, are you okay?"

"Yeah, it's gone. I'll be fine."

But then Barry started, and the rest of us laughed. "You got sick from watching Butch, you pansy."

Barry heaved for another five minutes. We then picked Butch and Barry out of the ditch, put their arms over our shoulders, and helped them the rest of the way home.

"We better not tell our parents about this or they won't let us go back."

"Do you think it was the water?"

"Coulda been, but the rest of us didn't get sick."

"Do ya think it was poison?"

"Nah. If it was poison, Butch and Berry would be dead. You guys don't feel like your gonna die, do ya?"

"No."

Then, some words of advice for Barry: "Tell your brother the pills don't work"

~ ~ ~

That fall we returned to Elementary School. I was in third grade and Butch was in fourth. Neither of us had much interest in school, so we quickly fell behind. Dad wasn't there to make us do our homework, Mom was in the hospital, and Mrs. Elkins just wanted us out of the house until it was time for bed. That suited us just fine.

In third grade, the emphasis was on reading. Each day we would be organized into groups based on our reading levels.

"I want John, Mary, Beth, Terry, Sally, Andrew, and Sue to work with me here in the front of the class. You're the Cardinals," my teacher, Mrs. Anderson, would say.

"Jay, Thomas, Martha, Sandy, Billy, Fran, Mike, and Debbie, you be here in the middle of the classroom. Miss Francis will work with you. You're the Robins."

"Joseph, Bob, Judy and Kobe, you'll be in the back of the classroom working with Mrs. Swartz, Bob's mom. You're the Blue Jays."

Mrs. Anderson took a lot of pride in the Cardinals and their achievements and did her best to turn the Robins into Cardinals. She encouraged us Jays to work hard to become Robins. We all knew who and what the Blue Jays were: the slow kids. I envisioned a day when I would be the only Blue Jay in the tree.

"You're a Blue Jay, you can't read." taunted Terry as we gathered on the playground under the basketball net.

"Yeah, but you're a sissy," I said.

"And you're a son-of-a-bitch," Terry declared.

I had heard that phrase before. Back in Cincinnati, a boy in kindergarten had called me that. Later I asked Dad, "What's a son-of-a-bitch?"

"Where did you hear that?"

"A boy at school called me one."

"That's a bad word, and you shouldn't be using it."

"But what is it?"

"A bitch is a girl dog, so it means that your mother is a dog. I'm sure the boy heard it at home and had no idea what it meant."

I let it go back in kindergarten, but no sissy was going to call my mom a dog and get away with it. Not today.

I found Terry and punched him as hard as I could directly in the nose. I had learned from fighting with Butch that when you hit someone in the nose, you take the life out of them.

There is no fight left. The only question was, "How much more am I going to beat you?"

Terry's nose immediately started bleeding and then I took him to the ground and continued hitting his face. I didn't hate Terry; we were friends. We played football together and sometimes he came over to play Kick the Can. But this wasn't Terry. This was some kid that had called my mom a dog.

"Stop it! You're killing him!"

One of the teachers pulled me off while I struggled to keep swinging. I was dragged to the principal's office with Terry's blood on my shirt and hands. I was exhibiting the behavioral pattern of a blue jay. Other birds don't mess with Blue Jays.

I would continue to fight like this through elementary school and into junior high. I spent a lot of time in the principal's office and my reputation grew. It wasn't until I joined the football team in ninth grade that this aggressive behavior was channeled in a different direction.

Mom had been in the hospital for six months and I started hearing Dad use the word *cancer* a lot. Our housekeepers were staying over the weekends now so we didn't see much of Dad either. Even when he was around, he was preoccupied. He couldn't replace the love that Mom had given Butch and me and it showed. He was our Dad but he wasn't really there. Butch and I were two boys with no direction, no structure, no discipline, and, worst of all, no love.

The only way we could get anyone to pay attention to us was to get into a fight, talk back to an adult, or terrorize another neighborhood kid.

# Chapter Four
## My Mother Doesn't Love Me

On the evening of May 2, 1953, Dad surprised us with a question: "How would you boys like to go to the hospital and see your mother? I've made arrangements with one of the nurses to sneak you into her room. We'll go tomorrow night on Butch's birthday. We'll celebrate Butch's birthday with Mom."

He emphasized that it was against the rules for kids to be in the hospital. "The two of you are going to have to behave. Do you understand?"

Butch and I assured Dad that we understood and that he could count on us.

We were excited. We hadn't seen Mom in over five months, and we were going on Butch's birthday. We'd have a party! "It'll be like in Cincinnati," Butch said.

We took a bath, put on our best clothes, got in the car, and drove to the hospital. Dad took us in the back door and climbed the steps to the third floor, then walked down a long hallway and into a hospital room. Mom was propped up in her bed in a sitting position. She looked great; her auburn curls hung to her shoulders, accenting her slim features. She wore her glasses and extended her arms to welcome us.

"Hi, boys. Come on up here with me."

She was surrounded by strange machines and hooked up to a variety of wires and tubes. One of the machines kept beeping.

Dad lifted Butch and me up onto the bed so we could sit on either side of her. She asked us about school and if we'd added to our fort.

I pulled myself in close so that I could feel the warmth of her body, her hair and her face. Although she was much thinner than I remembered, she still looked and smelled like my mom. She loved me. I knew she'd be home soon and that she'd be okay.

We laughed as she tickled us like she always had. We were having fun.

"Hold it down, boys," Dad warned us. "Remember, you're not supposed to be up here. We don't want to get caught."

"Mom, do you know what day this is?" Butch asked.

"It's Saturday, why?"

"No, what else is today?"

"I don't know. What else is today?"

"You don't know?" Butch asked with sudden sadness in his voice.

He slid off the bed and moved toward the door.

"What's wrong with him?" Mom asked.

"It's his birthday," Dad explained.

Butch turned and shouted, "You forgot my birthday! You don't care about us anymore. Why don't you come home?"

Mom was crushed, but she was also angry. Not at Butch but at her situation and what it was doing to her family.

"I am sorry, Butch. It's not like I don't have a lot of other things on my mind. I just forgot." Her voice was filled with both anger and embarrassment. "And believe me, I wish I could come home and be with you boys."

"Then why don't you?" Butch shouted back, with tears in his eyes. "Why can't I have a birthday party like the other kids?"

"Butch! Stop it!" Dad said.

"I can't come home. I don't know if I'll ever come home," Mom shouted back.

Butch only heard the anger in her voice. He had expected a party, but instead his mother had forgotten his birthday. More importantly, it showed she wasn't there for us anymore. We missed her and the way our life used to be. Butch stood by the door and pouted. I continued to sit with Mom.

Dad went over and tried to comfort Butch. "We can have your party. Come back over to your mom."

"No, I don't want a party here. I want to go home," he said through tears. "Let's all go home."

"We can't go home now. We came to visit Mom," he tried to explain.

"No, I want to go home now."

Tension filled the room and I held on tight to Mom. I was here, she was here, and Butch was being a baby.

"Please get down, Kobe," Mom said, motioning to my father to help me from the bed. "Dad and I have to talk."

What I didn't know is that this would be our last conversation with Mom. The last touch, the last smell, the last warmth we would experience.

Butch and I stood by the door while our parents talked. Dad didn't seem happy. He seemed scared and that wasn't like him. Mom seemed sad but not scared, so I figured things were fine. They were discussing sending Butch and me to Cincinnati next week, after school let out for summer vacation.

"Baby," I whispered to Butch, and turned away.

My brother hit me as hard as he could in the back of the head. My face slammed into the wall and I cried.

"Stop crying, Kobe, or I'll send you to the car," Dad commanded.

"Butch hit me," I yelled through my tears.

"He asked for it, Dad."

"Butch is always hitting me, Dad." I began to cry even louder, our voices now filling the hospital room where we weren't supposed to be.

"I'm going to send the two of you to the car," Dad threatened again.

"No, don't send Kobe to the car," my Mom interrupted. "I want to see him cry. Come over here Kobe, where I can see you."

I cried louder and harder. Her words stung much more than the hit Butch gave me. My mom wants to see me cry because she doesn't love me anymore, I thought.

Again, Mom spoke. "Come closer, over here by the side of the bed."

"You boys step out in the hall," Dad said, trying to cut the conversation off. "I'm taking you back to the car."

"No. Kobe come over here where I can see you," Mom said sharply.

"Kay, stop. You're scaring him."

Dad was right. I was scared. Butch opened the door and walked into the hall. I was frozen. I didn't know what to do and pressed my back tighter against the wall.

Suddenly Mom yelled out. "*You* stop! You don't know how I feel. You haven't even been here that much. Where have you been spending your nights?"

"Kay, settle down. I've been looking after the boys, you know that."

"I know no such thing, but I have my suspicions."

"As far as you're concerned," Mom continued, "I'm already…"

"Kay, that's enough." Dad grabbed me by the arm and took me to the door.

"Kobe, you come back here."

I looked over my shoulder and Mom was holding her face in her hands, crying.

I would live with this moment for the rest of my life, asking myself again and again, *Why did my mother want to see me cry? Why were they yelling at each other?* I couldn't stop crying. I didn't understand. The more Dad told me to stop, the harder I cried.

Dad walked us down the hall, marched down the staircase, dragged us to the car, and put us in the back seat. I leaned against the door and sobbed. Butch was silent.

About a half-hour later, Dad returned and drove us home. He never discussed what happened that night, and I never said anything to him or anybody else. I just kept wondering: "Why did my mom want to see me cry?"

# Chapter Five
## Live with Love

I was born on September 5, 1944, at 4:15 p.m. and delivered by Dr. Giles DeCourcy. My mother entered Good Samaritan Hospital on September 4 and left on September 15 with her second son. I had blond hair and blue eyes, weighed eight pounds, ten ounces, and was twenty-one inches long. The bill for my birth was $94.18. The church paid $74 and my parents owed $20.18.

Mom brought me to her mother's home at 514 Church Street in Saint Bernard, Ohio, a small industrial town just north of Cincinnati. Dad was stationed overseas and didn't learn of my birth until September 24. I have only fond memories of life in Saint Bernard where we lived until I was 7 years old. We lived in a working-class neighborhood with my maternal grandmother, Grandma Talon. We didn't have much but we had few expenses and fewer needs.

I didn't know my Grandfather Talon, who died before I was born. He must have done well for himself, though, because his home and neighborhood was nice by our standards. The two-story white clapboard house had a fenced-in back yard full of flowers, a stone fishpond, and an arbor. A porch stretched across the full front of the house and a swing hung on one end.

The front door opened to a large foyer with steps on the right leading upstairs to three bedrooms and a bathroom. Grandma Talon had one of the rooms; it was equipped with a small kitchen. The downstairs living and dining rooms had hardwood floors covered with area rugs. The dining room had a large two-pane window that looked directly into the neighbor's house just six feet away where our friends Ann and Mary lived.

The first floor also had a good-sized kitchen, a dining table, a full bath, and an enclosed back porch. Mom and Dad slept in what used to be the dining room and Butch and I slept on two steel cots in the former back porch. When Rooney arrived, he slept in a crib next to my parent's bed. Instead of a refrigerator, we had an ice box. A man would come twice a week to fill it with a big block of ice. On the right side of the house, steps led down to the cellar. Grandma kept her electric clothes-washer down here but she didn't have a dryer. Instead, she would hang our wash on a line in the side yard.

I remember that washer well because one day Butch convinced me to play with the ringer rollers.

"Put your fingers in there and see what happens."

"No, it'll eat my hand."

Still, my fingers danced near the menacing machine.

"You're a sissy if you don't do it." He challenged me, and I gave in.

The rollers grabbed my fingers, pulling my hand behind them. My fingers emerged on the other side, but the rollers squeezed my arm.

I screamed, "Stop it! Stop it!"

Butch pulled the plug and helped me reclaim my arm.

"Why'd you do that? Are you stupid?"

"You told me to. You dared me to."

Grandma Talon hollered down the clothes chute. "What are you boys doing?"

Butch held a finger in front of his mouth signaling for me to be quiet. "Nothing, Grandma," he yelled back. "We're OK."

Then he whispered, "Don't say anything. You may have broken Grandma's washing machine, but I won't tell. Let's get out of here."

Grandma Talon was a round lady, neither fat or big. She had a round face, wore round, wire-rimmed glasses, and had white hair with round curls and round edges over the rest of her body. She was a quiet, efficient grandma. She kept an orderly house and was always looking after Butch or me. She had milk toast every morning for breakfast, a dish composed of toast, butter, cinnamon, and sugar and served in a bowl with milk.

She also had coffee with lots of cream. I didn't like the milk toast but I did like her coffee. "Just a little Kobe," she'd say. "You shouldn't be drinking coffee."

Although Grandma Talon lived on the second floor, she had most of her meals with us in the kitchen. She spent hours tending to her flower and vegetable gardens, and she always wore gloves. "I work in a hospital where everything has to be clean, and I can't go to work with dirt under my fingernails," she explained many times.

She had other sayings, too.

"You have no reason to be afraid of bugs. You're bigger than them, so they're afraid of you. But remember, they are God's creatures."

"Keep yourself clean. Nobody likes being around a stinky boy."

"Little boys are to be seen and not heard. Speak when you are spoken to."

Our world was our neighborhood, our extended family, and the Catholic Church. We went to confession once a week, took communion every Sunday, and never ate meat on Friday. But I didn't mind. Being Catholic made me feel a part of something.

Half of my education came from my parents and the other half came from the church or, more specifically, the nuns. They introduced me to God, Jesus, and the Holy Ghost, which was a dove as far as I could tell from the pictures in prayer books. It was important to pray to this trio who were really one person, known as "God." Jesus was God's only son who was sent to Earth to save us from our sins. Jesus did that by dying on the cross. That was about it. If there was anything else I didn't understand, I was to accept it on faith.

We learned that it was important to go to confession and tell all your sins to the priest because if you died with sins on your soul, you faced either purgatory or hell. A mortal sin guaranteed hell, but you had to kill someone to go for that. If you had a lot of venial sins on your soul, you would have to spend time in purgatory before ascending to heaven.

We also learned that once you reached heaven, you lived with God and all the other people in heaven. You waited until the living people you loved died and joined you. Even those of us still on Earth got involved. We could help those in purgatory by saying prayers for them. That could get them in heaven ahead of schedule. As a child who didn't know anyone who had died, I offered my prayers, hoping to help them out.

I had to watch out for my own sins, though, particularly lying, cursing, talking back to Mom and Dad, or having "bad thoughts." I lived a pretty clean life at this point but the nuns said I couldn't go to confession and say that I hadn't done anything wrong, so I made things up. I would confess to a lie or having two bad thoughts, although I still wasn't sure what a bad thought was.

I also didn't understand the crucifixion. How could God allow people to be so mean to his son Jesus? If he was so all-powerful, why didn't he stop them? The nuns even said that God knew beforehand that they were going to be mean to him, which confused me even more.

I asked Mom about it. "God has a master plan that we don't always understand, and we have to have faith in him," she counseled. She told me about her brother Jimmy who had been a nice boy and a good student but died in a car accident in 1940 when he was only eighteen. "God wanted Jimmy in heaven with him," she said, "so he took him early."

Both my parents' families lived in Cincinnati -- no one had ever moved away. Dad was one of five kids, the oldest son. Mom was one of two children and was very close to her mother. Grandma Talon was by herself, and Mom was all the family she had left. Her husband had died years ago.

As I've said, her house on Church Street left me with some happy memories. It was on a hill, and when it rained, water would rush down the gutters. Butch and I would sit under them and let the water run over us. It was the closest thing we had to a swimming pool. Mom and Grandma Talon would sit on the front porch and watch for lightning. As soon as they saw some, we had to run inside.

Sometimes Mom would put on her swimsuit and sit alongside us, letting the water run over her feet.

In the winter, Mom, Butch, and I would build a snowman in the front yard. He was a dead ringer for Frosty the Snowman, before Frosty became popular, and we'd keep him up as long as possible. He had a carrot nose, coal for eyes, and one of Grandfather Talon's old hats. We'd stick branches in his side for arms.

I got pneumonia in the summer of 1948 and had to spend two months in bed. Mom and Dad moved my cot from the back porch to next to their bed. A doctor would come by the house once a week to check on me. I was pretty sick and my parents pretty scared but I enjoyed all the attention. Still, I was mad that Butch got to go outside and play every day while I was stuck in bed.

We didn't have a television, so evenings were spent on the front porch or in the living room in front of the radio. Butch and I liked "Jack Armstrong–the All American Boy" and, as we got older, "The Shadow." Later in the evening my parents and Grandma would listen to "Jack Benny," "Charlie McCarthy," and "Lux Radio Theater." During baseball season, I'd fall asleep many nights as Dad and Grandma listened to Cincinnati Reds' games. Mom wasn't interested in baseball but Grandma Talon sure was. She knew every player, their batting average, and position.

In 1948 we got our first television, a black-and-white with a five-inch screen. During the day, it showed a test pattern since nothing was on. At 7 p.m. it would light up. We'd invite neighbors into our living room to watch "The Original Amateur Hour." We had heard the show on the radio for years, and now there it was before our eyes! Within months we were watching "Kukla, Fran and Ollie" followed by "The Howdy Doody Show." Mom even bought Butch and me Buffalo Bob shirts which immediately became our favorite piece of clothing.

During the summer, the movie theater on Greenlee Avenue would show serials every Wednesday afternoon. Mom would walk Butch and me there to buy our tickets and a piece of candy and sit us down. "Now you stay here and watch the movie," she'd tell us. "I'm going to the grocery store to do some shopping. I'll be back to get you when the movie is over. Do you have to go to the bathroom before I go?"

Butch and I looked forward to Wednesday. Over the years, we saw all the *Superman, Flash Gordon,* and *Gene Autry* serials. We'd return the next week and the story would continue where it left off, always with the hero in the lurch.

Mom would pick us up and we'd walk back down Greenlee, each holding on to her shopping basket.

# Chapter Six
## Prayer Will Save My Mother

The weekend after we visited Mom in the hospital, we found ourselves back in Cincinnati with Grandma Grinkmeyer. She lived in a row house with a driveway on the side where we would play. Her house was in the old part of the city, close to where my grandfather worked at the Formica plant. When you entered the house, you walked into the living room. Behind it was the bedroom, behind that the dining room, and then the kitchen, with a bathroom on the side. A set of steep steps led from the bedroom upstairs to two more bedrooms. There was no bathroom upstairs. Heat drifted up from a coal furnace in the basement.

Aunt Ruthie and Grandma had been caring for Rooney and now they had Butch and me. We spent our days with Grandma or swimming with Diane Mason, our cousin. Her brother Tom was off studying to become a priest.

After my aunt got off work, she would take us with her shopping or for a walk. We always seemed to end up in Saint Pious Church. Butch and I were each given a rosary. Aunt Ruthie would tell us, "Pray for your mom. Jesus loves you. Jesus loves your mom. Pray to Jesus and his mother, the Virgin Mary, to make your mom better so that she can come home and be with you. You boys keep your rosary in your pockets so you can pray to Jesus anytime. When you get up in the morning, before you go to bed, or during the day, pray to Jesus. Jesus will make your mom better."

At Saint Pious Church we would kneel on the hardwood runners and say an entire rosary. The "Our Fathers" were to God and the "Hail Marys" were to Jesus' mother. We were never to pray directly to Jesus. He was too busy to receive our prayers directly. The Virgin Mother, we were told, would speak to Jesus for us.

"Mary mother of Jesus, my mom's in a hospital in Champaign and she's real sick," I would whisper to myself. "Would you please speak to Jesus and have him ask God to make her better so that she can come home to us?"

We attended church every Sunday. The endless kneeling, standing up, and sitting down got old. It didn't help that the priest spoke in Latin. But we always stayed after Mass and said an extra rosary for Mom.

"OK boys, come with me," Grandma would say, taking our hands and leading us to the front of the sanctuary. It was a massive building with stained-glass pictures in every window. Our shoes slapped out echoes on the marble floors. As we approached the altar, I could see Jesus hanging from the cross in front of us. He died for our sins and now he would make Mom better, I knew. We weren't alone though. A few people remained in the pews, bent over in urgent prayer. They too must have sick people they are praying for, I figured.

Grandma would then stop. "Genuflect." I dropped to my right knee, and then stood back up. It showed respect to Jesus. "And cross yourself."

Then we all began to murmur: "Name of the Father, the Son, and the Holy Ghost." Our right hands traced a line from forehead to left shoulder to right shoulder and down to our belly buttons. "Amen."

"We're going to light a candle for your mother," Grandma would say as we made a right turn toward the side of the church, which held stands with little candles in glass cups. She gave Butch and me a nickel or dime to drop in a small box, which clanged on the bottom. She picked up a thin stick, held the tip above an already burning candle, and lit a new one. Finally, she blew out the flame on the stick.

"Can I light one?" I always asked.

"No, only one," she said.

"I want to light one," I would say again, eyeing the rows of unlit candles. There was no priest saying "Limit one candle," and if I had to drop to my knees on this hard marble floor for the next three minutes to pray, I should at least get to light my own candle.

"No, only one," she told me again.

By the time we left, the church was always empty.

I looked forward to climbing down the church steps, though. Grandma would dig out a nickel to buy a pretzel the size of a small pizza for Butch and me to share. It was hot, doughy, and coated with crunchy salt crystals. It made going to church worth all the pain to my knees. Almost.

One Sunday was special, though, which Grandma and Aunt Ruthie made very clear. Butch, Rooney, and I all had our hair slicked down. We'd taken baths the night before, though we didn't know why.

"Something special's going to happen this morning," Auntie Ruthie told us. What could it be? Was I going to get to light my own candle? I knew my grandmother well enough. Surely not.

Halfway through the Mass, Aunt Ruthie nudged Butch and me. "Pay attention, now." Rooney was a toddler. He would always pay attention to anyone giving him any attention.

The priest finished his story. It was about a group of people who looked back at the city they were leaving when told not to and as punishment were turned into salt. Then he said, "I have a request for prayers for Kay Talon Grinkmeyer, who is in the hospital with cancer in Champaign, Illinois. She needs your prayers so that she can come home to her family."

Butch's eyes bulged. This was a good sign. The church was packed. No one had left early. Everyone was praying for Mom, praying directly to Jesus – not through Mary, his mother – but directly to Jesus. Even the priest asked Jesus to make our mom better. Grandma had told us priests that were next to God in holiness.

"Lord, hear our prayers," the priest finally said. Everyone in the church responded, "Amen." And that was it. I looked up and Auntie Ruthie gave me a big toothy smile. I looked at Grandma and her head was still down, saying the final amen.

How could Jesus not hear all these people? Mom would soon be home.

Why hadn't we done this six months ago? I wondered. But it was done now. Finally.

We left the church, headed down the steps, and walked past the pretzel man. I didn't care. The whole church had just prayed to Jesus. He was the son of God. He could give us our mom back. I didn't need a salty pretzel today.

# Chapter Seven
## What About Our Agreement with God?

Kay Talon Grinkmeyer died on July 14, 1953. She was 30 years old. I was eight. Butch was ten. Rooney was two.

Butch and I had been in Cincinnati since school ended. Dad had returned to Champaign to look after Mom. On this particular July afternoon, Butch and I were playing in the driveway and Aunt Ruthie was looking after Rooney.

Dad drove up. "Hi, boys." Instantly, all three of us were at his feet, clinging at his legs, not wanting to let him go. After a few minutes and several pats on the head, he went into the house, leaving the three of us on the driveway with Auntie Ruthie.

When he was three steps up to the porch, he turned back to us. "Butch and Kobe, come into the house. I need to talk to you."

Aunt Ruthie stayed outside with Rooney.

I knew what it was: He's going to tell us when Mom was coming home and when Butch, Rooney, and I were going back to Champaign to all be together again. I ran up the steps and followed him into the house, grabbing his leg as he moved toward the sofa. Butch lagged behind, entering the door with his head down, hands held together over his belly button. I looked up at Dad and his face was sad as he watched Butch approach the sofa.

We both sat down, Dad in the middle between Butch and me.

I remember that moment as if it were yesterday. The sofa set against the side wall. It was brown and the fabric was soft and fuzzy, like short-cropped hair on a dog. Although it was the middle of the afternoon, the end table lights were on and the curtains were pulled shut. Dad wore brown slacks, a sports coat and a tie, not his normal attire. I could hear Grandma Grinkmeyer in the kitchen and the traffic outside. Like always, the smell of food filled the house.

Dad put an arm around each of us and pulled us close. "Boys, Mom died two days ago."

*Mom died,* I repeated to myself. *What does that mean?*

The priest at Saint Thomas Aquinas had said that when you die, you either go to heaven or hell. Heaven, if you've been good and followed all the rules; hell if you've been bad, where there's fire and the devil. That's why it's so important to confess your sins to a priest when you've been bad or they'll stay on your soul and God will see them when you try to get into heaven. Did Mom go to confession before she died? She was a good person. I hope they didn't feed her meat in the hospital on Friday and that she didn't tell anyone a lie. Surely she'll go to heaven. The nuns said that the dead wait in heaven for us. What will she do while she's waiting? What will I do without Mom? Will I have to stay here in Cincinnati with Rooney and Grandma? My mind moved so fast that I didn't feel anything. I didn't know what to do.

I leaned forward and looked at Butch. He was crying, but it wasn't a normal cry. He didn't make any sounds but tears were coming out of his eyes. I didn't understand why. He laid over on Dad's leg and Dad held him. I looked at Dad and he had tears in his eyes. I was the only one who didn't.

"We're having Mom's funeral tomorrow," Dad said.

I still didn't know what to say but knew my dad expected something from me, some kind of reaction. But I had nothing to give. I felt nothing.

Finally, I spoke. "What's a funeral?" I knew what a funeral was. We had lived next to a cemetery in Saint Bernard and I had seen workers dig a hole in the ground and put in a box with a person in it. When the people left, a worker would return to fill up the hole with dirt. Then they put the grass back on the mound of dirt and placed a gravestone at the top of the hole. But I asked anyway. "What's a funeral?" I hoped I was wrong.

"A funeral is a ceremony at the church that we hold before we bury Mom at the cemetery."

"The cemetery by Grandma Talon's house?"

"No, another cemetery."

Butch was still crying, clinging to Dad's leg.

Mom has died and she won't be coming home, I thought. My mind began to race even faster. This is scary, I thought. I need to get away. I don't understand. I've seen mice and snakes die. My stomach hurts. I hope I don't throw up like Butch did in the ditch.

I had to get out of the room. "Can I go back out to play?"

"Sure Kobe, you can go back out to play." Dad wiped his eyes with a handkerchief and reached over and held Butch.

I got up and walked across the room, opened the door, and stepped out on the porch into the sunlight. I closed the door and felt better but my mind continued to race. Mom died two days ago. I'll start back in school in a couple of months. Mom's funeral is tomorrow. I guess we won't be able to go swimming tomorrow.

I climbed down the three steps, Aunt Ruthie was crying, holding Rooney real tight. I stood next to her and she put her arm around me. I still didn't know what to do. It felt nice for Auntie Ruthie to hold me, but she wasn't Mom.

Then I began to get angry

How could she have died? We said the rosary every day. The people in the church prayed to Jesus. The priest asked Jesus to make Mom better so she could come home. She went to the hospital and the doctors worked hard to make her better. Everyone said she was going to be okay. All Butch and I had to do was pray. We did that.

Didn't we do the rosary right? Didn't I do it enough? Whose fault is this? Is it God's? Why didn't he send Mom home?

Butch came out the front door, his eyes red and swollen and his cheeks stained with tears. He approached Aunt Ruthie, dug into his pocket, took out his rosary, and threw it at her.

"It doesn't work," he yelled. "Jesus didn't send Mom home. You said that Jesus would hear our prayers. You lied. Jesus doesn't care about me."

Rooney started to cry, and Aunt Ruthie tried comfort him. "Butch, I'm sorry. God had other plans for your mom. God wanted your mom in heaven with him."

I reached into my pocket and put my rosary on the ground next to Aunt Ruthie. I pulled away from her and started to walk toward the house. I put my foot on the first step but there was nothing for me in there and turned to look for Butch.

I hope God lets Mom in heaven, I thought. He didn't let her come home. He didn't listen to our prayers. I hope he lets her in heaven. I hope Auntie Ruthie is right…this time.

Inside Grandma's house, another battle was being waged in the kitchen, and I stopped to listen. Our aunts and uncles were trying to decide who was going to take who – something they had tried to figure out weeks ago. Uncle Norb and Aunt Flo volunteered to take Butch home with them and raise him like their son with their daughter Sandy. Uncle Eddie and Aunt Sis said they would take me and raise me with their daughter Cherry. She was just a baby and I could be her older brother. Aunt Dee and Uncle Phil would take Rooney since they had only one son.

But Dad wasn't on board. "I promised Kay that I would keep the boys together," he said. "I'll be back for Butch and Kobe in a couple of weeks. After that, I'll come to get Rooney."

"Chuck, be realistic. How are you going to do that?" someone said. "Your boys need a mother and they need one now. You're not at home enough now to take care of them. They can't continue to be raised by housekeepers. They both already have problems."

"I'll get it handled. I'll take care of it."

"How?"

"I'll find them a mother."

"Who's going to marry you with three boys? Especially when two of them are wild!"

"I'll be back to get Rooney after I get married. Our family is going to stay together. I promised Kay. I don't want to talk about it anymore." And that was that.

The next morning everyone but Aunt Ruthie, Rooney, and me went to the funeral. They left early in the morning and didn't return until dinner. I spent most of the day in the backyard throwing stones at the big wall behind Grandma's house.

After the funeral, the house was full of people and everyone wanted to kiss me. Several told me I was cute. "I know you'll miss your mom," they'd say. Then they'd muss-up my hair. There was a lot of food and beer, even some pop, which we never had at home. It was just like a party.

I overheard someone say, "What's going to happen to those three boys? Sis said that Chuck is insisting that he take them back to Champaign."

"That's crazy! Those boys are at an age when they need a mother. There's no telling how they'll turn out without a mother's love, and if he remarries, there's still no guarantee. They need to stay in Cincinnati with family."

"I'm sure he'll reconsider and do what's right for those boys."

Butch and I ate what we wanted, then headed to the backyard, back by the stone wall. We each took a full bottle of pop. There was no telling when we would have this again.

"What happened at the funeral?" I asked.

Butch walked away like he didn't want to talk. Then he turned around and blurted out in an angry voice. "Mom was in a box, a coffin, in the front of the church. She looked like she was sleeping. There were a lot of people in the church. The priest did what he does at Sunday Mass. Dad took me up to the front after most of the people left and asked if I wanted to kiss Mom good-bye."

"Did you? Did you kiss her good-bye?"

"Yeah."

"What did she feel like?"

"Nothing, I guess. She felt like Mom, but not warm."

"Cold?'

"Yeah, cold, I guess"

"Then what?"

"The priest asked us to kneel on the floor and pray her into heaven. I wouldn't do it and I'll never do it again. It doesn't work. Jesus doesn't hear our prayers."

"What did Dad do?"

"He prayed."

"Did all the other people in the church pray?"

"Yeah, I guess."

"Then what?"

"Dad closed the lid on the coffin and another man locked it shut. Then Uncle Norb, Uncle Eddy, Uncle Phil, and some other men picked it up and took it out to a station wagon. Dad called it a hearse. We all got in cars and followed the station wagon to the cemetery where they put Mom and the coffin in the ground."

"Did the men come and fill the hole with dirt?"

"No, the priest asked all the people to pray, and Aunt Flo started crying real loud, and Uncle Nord had to take her to their car."

"Why did Aunt Flo cry so much?"

"I don't know, she just did," Butch said, and walked off.

Why did Aunt Flo cry so much? I thought. Did Mom like to see her cry, too? They were good friends, after all.

Butch went to the step at the base of the wall. I followed but kept a distance, at first, but soon went over and sat next to him. We didn't talk anymore about what had happened or the days that led up to today.

People were leaving the house, but some of them came over and mussed our hair one last time. Then a grasshopper hopped on my pant leg. I grabbed it in the palm of my hand and then held it with two fingers. It clawed at the air with its four front legs. Its big eyes looked at me, seeming to ask, *Why are you holding me? I wasn't hurting you. Let me go. Leave me alone. Please don't hurt me.*

Butch watched as I pulled off its two hind legs. It spit what looked like tobacco juice on my hand – maybe it was blood – and continued to claw at me with its four remaining legs. I threw his two legs into the grass. They didn't mean a thing to me and I wasn't going to put them back on the grasshopper. I was in control here.

I put him back down on the ground, back in his familiar world. It righted itself and turned, trying to figure out where it was. With its four front legs, the grasshopper pulled itself toward the grass. Butch and I bent over and watched its every move. Somehow it knew where to find the taller grass where it might be safe from birds. The grasshopper ignored us. It was adjusting to its loss. It was going to survive.

It stopped moving. Butch looked me in the eyes. "I think they can grow back their hind legs. He'll be okay."

We returned to the step and sat down. Slowly, I leaned on my brother, who took my weight. I wished he'd put his arm around me and tell me we'd be fine but he didn't. Maybe I should put my arm around him and tell him we'd be fine. But I didn't.

Finally he said, "We should have stayed in Saint Bernard, on Church Street."

I hurt inside. I wanted to cry like a baby but I couldn't allow that.

I leaned harder on Butch. "Would Mom have lived if we'd stayed on Church Street?"

"I don't know," Butch said. "I don't know."

# Chapter Eight
## Running Wild

The wake was finally over and everyone had left. Dad, Aunt Ruthie, and Grandma sat in the living room and reviewed the day. It was adult talk about how nice the service had been, how bad Uncle Somebody looked. It meant nothing to me, and eventually Grandma announced it was time for bed.

Rooney slept on a small cot in Grandma's room and Butch and I shared one of the upstairs bedrooms. We slept together in a double bed – a steel frame bed with springs topped by a mattress. We would start the night on either side of the bed but by morning would have sunk to the middle and were sleeping against each other. This morning we woke up wet.

"You wet the bed!" Butch accused.

"No, you wet the bed!" I shot back.

We both were right. It was something that neither of us had done for five years. We reported our accidents to Grandma and she had a ready explanation. "That's to be expected after what you boys have been through," she assured us. "I'm sure it won't happen again."

Grandma was a wise lady. She had raised five children of her own but was wrong on this one. Bedwetting would become a part of my life for the next four years. It would trigger many fights and be the source of much embarrassment and humiliation.

Butch and I spent the rest of the summer in Cincinnati. When September arrived, Dad had not yet come for us, so we started school at Saint Aloysius on Reading Road. It wasn't far from Grandma's house so we could walk. From the first day I knew that this would be different from Westview in Champaign. First off, it was run by nuns, and I knew what that was like after Saint Thomas Aquinas. Second, and most disturbing, about sixty kids emerged from the double doors of an old building next to the playground marching in two columns in perfect step. They were accompanied by a nun who would clap her hands and directing them to turn, stop, or start.

I saw them out the window while sitting in class the first morning of school. They made their way across the playground and into the school building. I could hear them marching down the hall toward our classroom. Then four claps and a group of seven boys and girls in blue pants or skirts and white shirts entered our room and took seats. Not a word was spoken and I wasn't about to voice all the questions running through my head. I remembered the feeling of a ruler across my outstretched hand even though it been three years.

At recess I found Butch. "Who are those kids?" I asked, pointing to the ones in the blue and white clothes.

"They're orphans. They live over there in that building."

"What are orphans?"

"Kids who don't have a mom or dad or anyone to take care of them."

"Are we going to be orphans?"

"I don't know."

"We're going back to Champaign to live with Dad, aren't we?"

"I don't know."

"We're not going to move into that building, are we?"

"I don't know."

"What do you know?"

"We're here now."

Two weeks later, Dad came and took Butch and me back to Champaign. Rooney stayed in Cincinnati with Grandma Grinkmeyer. Butch got madder and I got meaner, and our reputation continued to grow. We both continued to wet the bed.

Before all this, Butch and I rarely fought. We were best of friends, and he looked out for me. But now we were always fighting. We started hitting each other, trying to hurt each other. Since he was older and bigger, I usually got the worst of it.

For the next year, housekeepers came and went, normally starting on Monday and quitting by Friday when Dad returned. Sometimes Dad had to come home early in the week because they threatened to leave us alone. "I'm not spending another day with these animals," he'd be told.

The fighting got fiercer. It peaked that fall when Butch caught me using his baseball glove. He snatched it away from me. "Don't use my things. You have your own glove."

I mocked him. "Butchie Bulmer, take your stupid glove."

I don't remember where the label Butchie Bulmer came from but it infuriated him. He went into a rage and swatted me on the side of the head, knocking me to the ground. In a flash he was on top of me, hitting as hard as he could. "I hate you. I'm going to kill you."

He wore a Saint Christopher medal on a heavy chain around his neck. I grabbed the chain and twisted it, choking him while trying to fend off his blows with my arms. He was unable to breath and stopped hitting me as he grabbed at the chain. I wouldn't stop twisting and he rolled off to break my grip.

I got up, bent over, and hit him directly in the nose as he lay on the ground, gasping for air. His nose spirited blood, which was magnified by his heavy breathing, causing him to spray blood on his shirt. He rolled over on all fours to protect himself. I kneed him in the ribs and he collapsed onto his side. He continued gasping and regaining his breath, blood spraying from his mouth like an aerosol can. I mocked him. "Butchie Bulmer, Butchie Bulmmmmer." When he started to recover I took off. I ran for three blocks and hid behind the Swartz's house until it started to turn dark.

When I returned home, Butch and Mrs. Elkins were eating dinner. I pulled out my chair and sat down between them, filled my plate, and started to eat.

"I'm going to kill you," Butch growled. He still wore the blood-spattered shirt.

I didn't know if he meant right that moment or sometime in the future. I looked to Mrs. Elkins for protection but she kept eating and didn't take her eyes out of the magazine she was reading.

Butch didn't try to take my life so I assumed I would at least get a last meal and continued eating. And while he never did kill me, we continued to fight each other as well as other boys for years to come.

# Chapter Nine
## Meeting Grace

I was lying face down in the ditch next to the culvert, preparing to make a break for the can, when Dad called out. "Butch, Kobe, come in here. I have somebody I'd like you to meet."

We ran to the front door and stepped into our small living room. Sitting in the armchair was a lady. A table lamp shone next to her, and the light made it look like she filled the whole room. Mrs. Elkins was in the kitchen, peeking around the corner and listening to every word.

Dad was dressed to go out, wearing a sports shirt, slacks, and shiny brown shoes. His hair was combed back real neat. Aunt Ruthie had once told me that men get "slicked-up" to go out with ladies.

This lady didn't look like any of the housekeepers we had in the past. She had long thin legs, which were crossed, letting her knees show below her skirt. She wore a tight flowered dress, not one of those baggy ones like housekeeper wear. Her hair was dark and shiny and all done up. Her cheeks were red and so were her lips. She wore long earrings and she smelled good. She was smoking a cigarette and greeted us with a friendly smile. As she reached out to shake my hand, she said, "My name is Grace Plotner. Nice to meet you, Kobe."

I didn't know what to say, so I didn't say anything. She smiled again, looking at me like she knew me.

Dad spoke up. "Boys, I've been going out with Grace for several months now. She and I are going to get married. She'll be your new mom."

I turned to Butch, my mind flooded with questions. *Can you just go out and get a new mom. Is that allowed? What does he mean that they've been going out? She doesn't look like our mom or any of our friend's moms.* Butch was mute.

"What would you like to call her?" Dad asked.

I'm sure the conversation was longer than that, but that's all I remember. I looked back at Grace Plotner. She was a real lady with make-up and done-up hair. She had on silk stockings and high heels. She saw me looking and she smiled.

Butch broke the silence. "Mom, I guess. You said she was going to be our mom, didn't you?"

I thought Butch was about to cry.

"Yes, she's going to be your mom," Dad answered with a grin. Apparently he had expected a different reaction.

"Okay, then, we'll call her Mom," Butch stated, and looked at me.

I said nothing because I didn't understand. Is that how it works? One mother dies and then you go out and get a new one? I was empty. No one was saying anything. I wanted to cry but wasn't going to let that happen again like I cried in front of my mother at the hospital. I wanted to go back to the ditch. I wanted to hide.

"How about you, Kobe? Is Mom okay with you?" Dad asked.

I looked at Dad. He looked at me. I looked at Grace Plotner. She looked at me. I looked at Butch. He was looking at the floor. I looked at Mrs. Elkins. She looked back with a big full smile, nodding her head. I looked back at Dad, who was expecting an answer. I didn't have one for him. I wanted to crawl into the tall grass, like that grasshopper. These people were about to eat me and I needed to hide. This just wasn't right. We come back from Cincinnati and Mom is gone and her things are gone and now here's Grace Plotner, our new mom.

I heard my Dad's voice echoing in my head: "Your Mom is dead. She won't be coming home." So this is what happens next?

"How about you, Kobe? Dad repeated. "Is Mom okay with you?"

Butch came to my rescue. "Can we go back out and play?"

"Sure boys, you can go back out and play, but only for another half-hour. Mrs. Elkins will put you to bed. I'll see you in the morning."

So Mrs. Elkins is staying, I thought. I wondered how long she'd keep coming.

Once outside, Butch didn't say a thing about what just happened. We never talked about it, about this Grace Plotner, about getting a new mom, about our old mom. We didn't talk that night. We didn't talk after the wedding. We didn't talk about it for decades.

We returned to our game of Kick the Can. I found my place in the ditch where I felt safe and comfortable. I pulled my arms tight against my chest and closed my eyes. Maybe I could just stay here, I thought. I wondered if grasshoppers really do grow their hind legs back? I sure hoped they did.

As Sandy searched the neighbor's yard for another Hider, I sprung from the ditch and ran for the can. She spotted me and we raced. She was faster but she had more ground to cover. I focused on the can, timed my stride, and prepared to kick it, but suddenly the can flew up from the ground. Sandy had made it first. "You're It!" she hollered.

I didn't know it at the time, and I didn't come to realize it for many years, but that the lady we met that night, Grace Plotner, was about to change the path that Butch and I were on. She would do more to alter the direction of my life than anyone I encountered over the next fifty years. She would also be responsible for the biggest disappointment I would ever have in any of my relationships.

Grace Plotner and Charles H. Grinkmeyer were married on June 6, 1954. It was exactly ten years after D-Day, and we were about to face an invasion ourselves.

# Chapter Ten
## Alone at Camp and a Lesson in Humiliation

This was going to be a great summer. Butch and I were going to sleep-away camp. We had never been on a vacation, let alone camp. Our destination was Camp Anachegie in Wisconsin. I had no idea what camp would be like. I just knew I would be able to swim every day, paddle a canoe, and explore the woods. That excited me. One of the programs was called Cowboy Camp. Each camper was assigned a horse that he rode and took care of every day. I had watched cowboys on TV, seen them in the movies, played them in the yard, and now I was going to have the chance to be one for six weeks. I couldn't wait.

We received a camp brochure at home which Butch and I studied in detail. Dad explained that he and Grace would be going on a honeymoon after they were married to get to know each other better. That's why Butch and I would go to camp. This didn't really make sense, but I didn't care. I was going to camp!

On our drive north to camp, Butch and I didn't fight or taunt each other – a first. Before Grace's arrival, our family had the basics but little more. Vacations were things that other people took. I hadn't felt deprived, though. We'd always been active and had each other, so there were plenty of adventures. But this was going to be special.

As we drove, cornfields gave way to forests. I envisioned Camp Anachegie buried deep in the woods. As the miles rolled by, we kept asking Dad, "Are we there yet? Are we there yet?" Finally, somewhere north of Madison, Dad answered. "We're almost there, boys."

Five minutes later, Dad spotted a sign for the camp, and arrow pointing right. We turned down a dirt road lined with tall green trees. It wound up hills, down valleys, and across creeks. As we crested a hill, the forest opened up to a green pasture and a huge, sparkling blue lake surrounded by tall trees. At the edge of the lake stood several buildings made of logs next to a brown sandy beach. It was beautiful. Better than the brochure.

Butch and I were on the edge of the backseat leaning into the front, pointing and screaming. "Look at that! Canoes! Look down there to the right. Indian tepees!" Dad had a huge smile on his face.

We parked by the biggest building and jumped out. Butch and I immediately ran to the lake. One of the canoes was covered with birch bark, just like Indians had done in the movies. There were rowboats and a floating raft with a diving board on it. The water was roped off into swimming areas, and there was even a chair on stilts for the lifeguard.

I was a good swimmer – Dad had taught me in the river when we went fishing back in Cincinnati – and then I swam when my second cousin took us to a pool when we stayed with Grandma. I had seen the bigger kids use a diving board then. Maybe I'd become a diver at camp.

Dad hollered to us. "You boys go ahead and look around, but don't get in the water. I'm going to get you registered."

I wanted to keep exploring. "Where are the horses?" I asked Butch. "I don't see any horses. We will get to ride, won't we?"

"They're probably kept somewhere else, maybe over by the tepees. Don't worry about it."

Butch began skipping rocks across the lake. Each time they'd skip, he'd count out, "One, two, three."

I picked up a rock, leaned over a little to the side like he had, and threw it is hard as I could. Ker-plunk. I never could get even one skip.

"Who do you think lives in those tepees over there?" I asked Butch, knowing he didn't know anything more about it then I did. "Do you think they're real Indians?" But I was so excited, I wanted to know everything right then.

"I don't know," he replied and skipped another rock. "One, two, three, four."

"Okay, boys, come on over here," Dad called. "I've got you registered, but they won't be ready to take you to your campsites until three o'clock when the other campers arrive. Mrs. Elkins made some sandwiches for lunch, and then you'll have to wait a bit."

Dad and Grace Plotner were getting married the next week. With Butch and me at camp, and Rooney in Cincinnati with Grandma Grinkmeyer, they would have six weeks to themselves.

"No problem, Dad," Butch assured him. "We'll be fine. You go on. I'll look after Kobe."

Dad slapped us on the backs and told us to behave ourselves and have a good time. "See you in six weeks."

It was just past noon, so Butch and I sat down, where it looked like campers gathered for campfires, and had our lunch. Butch asked if I'd rather stayed in the Indian Village then the Cowboy Camp since I liked Indians so much.

"No, I think I'd rather be a cowboy," I answered between bites of a peanut butter and jelly sandwich. "I hope they don't give me one of those big horses. I'd rather have the small one, but not too small. Do you think real Indians live in those teepees?" I asked again.

After lunch we ran up and down the bleachers that climbed the hillside around the campfire. About an hour later, an older kid came over and introduced himself as Billy, one of the counselors.

Billy was about 18 and red-headed with a lot of freckles, just like Berry back home. His head had an odd shape, though, kind of flat on the sides and coming to a broad point on top. I would learn later that the other counselors called him "Canoe Head." He told us he was a college student and did this in the summer for college credit and he got paid, too.

Billy explained that each village had its own counselors and that he was assigned to Cowboy Camp this week. He said that if Butch would pick up his stuff, he'd helped him get settled over in Cowboy Camp. He could get first pick of the horses and his bunk.

"I'm going to Cowboy Camp too," I informed Billy.

"No, you're going to be in Eagles Nest."

"No, I'm with Butch. We're together. We're brothers and we're both signed up for Cowboy Camp. Our Dad just signed us up, but he had to go back to Champaign."

"No, I got the papers right here, and you're signed up for Eagles Nest. You have to be eleven-years-old to stay in Cowboy Camp, and it says here you're nine. So you can't be in Cowboy's Camp. There will be another counselor here in a few minutes to take you Eagles Nest."

Butch picked up his bag and looked at me. "You'll be okay. Maybe you can get in to Indian Village and sleep in a teepee."

"No, you have to be 10-years-old to stay in Indian Village," Billy explained, further dashing my hopes.

Butch and the counselor headed up a small path and disappeared into the woods. As they left, I felt something I had never felt before. I couldn't identify it at the time but I know now it was fear. I just knew it didn't feel good. My face tightened up and I felt tears in my eyes, but I couldn't cry. I wouldn't allow myself to cry.

I sucked my lower lip in-between my teeth and bit on it. I took a deep breath and said to myself, *You'll be okay. Butch said you'll be okay.* I sat back down on the bench and kept repeating to myself, *You'll be okay. You'll be okay.*

Dad had told us we'd stay together. He had expected us to stay together. He was going to be mad at these people when he found out. I wished he was here now. He'd get me into Cowboy Camp.

About twenty minutes later, another young guy approached me and hollered, "Are you Kobe Grinkmeyer? Come with me. We're going to Eagles Nest." I grabbed my stuff and followed him up the hill. He seemed happy and glad to see me. I could feel some of the pain slipping away. I started to believe I'd be okay.

We climbed up the hill. About halfway up, he said, "My name is Nathan. Let me help you with your bag." He reached down and took it.

Nathan appeared to be a college student but looked more like a camp counselor than Billy. He was close to six-feet tall with dark, wavy hair and a good tan. His head was round like it was supposed to be.

"You're in the new building," he said, "and since you're the first one here, you can choose any bed you want."

There were two cinderblock buildings with tin roofs and Nathan led me to the one on the right. Inside were rows of bunk beds with an open area in the center and what looked like a bathroom in the back.

"If I were you, I'd take one near the back so you don't have to walk so far to the bathroom in the middle of the night. And I'd take a lower bunk so you don't have to climb up and down all week."

I did as Nathan suggested and threw my suitcase on a lower bunk. "I'm going to be here for six weeks," I corrected him.

"Six weeks? Are you sure?"

"Yeah, my brother and I are here for six weeks. He's in Cowboy Camp. I was supposed to be in Cowboy Camp," my voice suddenly weak, "so I'll probably be moving soon." I stopped with that so I wouldn't cry.

"Well, okay, you can just hang around here. The other campers should be arriving in about half an hour. I have to do some things at the administration building but I'll check back on you later. I'll look into that Cowboy Camp mix-up."

Nathan walked out the door and I looked around the empty building, which seemed nice enough, but that feeling had returned. Again, I sucked my lower lip in-between my teeth and bit. I opened my suitcase, took out a pair of socks, and put them up to my face. They smelled like home. I took out an old T-shirt worn thin. Mrs. Elkins had wanted to throw it away in the rag bag but I wouldn't let her. I rubbed it up and down my arm and it made me feel better. I wondered what Butch was doing now and if he missed me as much as I missed him. I started to cry, but I couldn't.

"Men don't cry," Dad had said when he was in the war. Even when his buddies were killed right next to him, he didn't cry. "If you don't cry when you see your buddies die, you don't cry over small things," he told us.

This didn't feel like a small thing to me, so I bit my lip harder. But men don't cry over small stuff and nobody is getting killed here, I reasoned. Besides, Nathan is looking into it for me.

A half hour later, the building started to fill up with other campers just as Nathan said it would. As each group came in, they would scramble for their beds, laughing and hollering. It seemed like most of them already knew each other. I later learned they did because many came from church groups and school groups. Within an hour the building was full.

A boy named Brett took the bunk above mine. He seemed like a nice guy. He was part of a church group and knew a lot of the other boys. He asked me my name and introduced me to his friends. I put my socks and T-shirt back in the suitcase and followed Brett around.

I was fine, just like Butch said I would be. But why didn't he come with me to Eagles Nest? Maybe they didn't allow ten-year-olds here. That must be it.

Nathan stuck his head in the door and hollered, "It's dinner time, guys. Follow me."

About forty of us – boys from both buildings – started walking down the hill toward a long, narrow building called the Mess Hall. Inside I found long tables with melamine plates, plastic glasses, and silverware. I just stayed with Brett. We all got in a line and the older guys put food on our plates. When we returned to our table, Nathan pointed to a pitcher in the middle. "There's the bug juice. If you want milk, it's in the machine up front."

Brett didn't get milk, so I didn't either. I drank the bug juice, a sickly-sweet drink like Kool-Aid.

After dinner, we played outside our building, climbing ropes and running through the woods. We found a chin-up bar and I was pretty good. I could chin myself more times than any of Brett's friends. I started to feel part of the group.

As it started to get dark, Nathan told us to get ready for the campfire. "Put on a jacket. It will get cold tonight. And bring your flashlights because it will be *real* dark when we come back." Then he gave us a warning. "Don't turn on your flashlight at campfire or it will be taken away for the rest of the week."

I ran to my suitcase and got my metal flashlight. I had never owned one before. We always had to use someone else's when we played kick the can. But the brochure had been very clear: Each camper had to bring a flashlight. I had wanted to use it at home but Dad wouldn't let me, correctly guessing that I would wear out the batteries. After all, I was going to need it for six weeks.

We all marched to the campfire area. There must have been 100 boys, all sitting in a big horseshoe going up ten rows around a big bonfire. All the counselors were introduced and each one described some of the things we would be doing over the next week. We sang songs, both church songs and camping songs. Then one of the counselors told a ghost story. It was scary but it was fun.

I saw Butch on the other side of the campfire with his group. They didn't have cowboy hats or cowboy boots that I could see, but he seemed to be having a good time, too.

The head counselor explain that the bugle would blow at 7:30 in the morning and we were to brush our teeth and head down to the lake in our underwear and flip-flops for a bath. After the bath, we would return to our cabins to get dressed and then go to breakfast.

Nathan gathered us together and we headed back to Eagles Nest with our flashlights glowing. There was a lot a lot of laughing and kidding, mouth farts, armpit farts, and just general 10-year-old boy fun. Nathan told us to get ready for bed. I went to the bathroom, got into my PJs, and crawled into my bunk. Overall, it had been a good day, more ups then downs, and I felt I would be okay. Off in the distance, I heard a bugle playing taps, and I thought: This is neat; this is really camp. And I fell asleep.

In the morning I was awakened by the sound of the bugle and Nathan screaming, "Hit the deck! Time to get up! On the beach in five minutes in your underwear and flip-flops."

Although I was awake, I didn't move. I didn't open my eyes. I hoped I was dreaming, that I was home on Patricia Court. I don't want to be at camp, I thought to myself. How could this have happened? I went to the bathroom before I went to bed. I didn't drink any water. I only had one glass of bug juice. I did just like Dad told me to do. Why did this happen to me?

I had wet the bed. I didn't know what to do. If I got up, other boys would see my PJs all wet. They would smell me and they would laugh. They wouldn't like me anymore. It wouldn't matter that I could do more chin-ups. They would think I was a baby, because, after all, I wet the bed like a baby.

I pushed by face deep in the pillow. At home I knew how to deal with this. Dad and Butch had grown to expect this every morning. I closed my eyes tight and asked God to take this away this cold, wet feeling. I had learned to live with this smell at home but was not prepared to share it with strangers. I was ashamed. I was alone. And I was here for six weeks.

Again I asked God to take it away. I didn't pray to Jesus or Mary anymore. They had let me down when it really counted. I spoke to God directly. I closed my eyes tight and prayed. "Please, God, make this go away and never come back again." Nothing happened. I was still wet and cold.

Where was Butch? Why wasn't he here? Why wasn't I at Cowboy Camp with him?

Brett poked me. "Kobe, it's time to get up. Wake up."

"Okay, I'm getting up." I rolled over on my back. Now my butt was wet, too. Brett moved off to the bathroom and I quickly got out of bed, grabbed some clean underwear, and stuffed my PJs under the blankets. I hope they don't smell it, I thought to myself. I hope it dries before tonight. I hope it doesn't happen again. God, please don't let this happen again. I slipped on my flip-flops and followed Nathan down to the beach. Although I wore the evidence, no one seemed to notice. No one seemed to smell me. Maybe I would be okay.

At lakeside, everyone stripped off their underwear, set them on top of their flip-flops, grabbed a bar of soap, and ran into the cold lake. It crossed my mind that the maybe the reason we were doing this was that everybody had wet the bed last night.

The days at Camp Anachegie were full of swimming, canoeing, nature hikes, crafts, and just plain fun. But each night after campfire I would crawl into a wet, smelly bed and hope that it would remain my secret until the end of the week. It was wet in the middle of the mattress so I would try to stay to the side. Each night the smell got worse and I feared that the other boys would detect it. I prayed to God and my dead mom to look over me and not let it happen again.

On the third morning, as I was coming back from the lake bath, Nathan grabbed my arm. "Come outside with me, Kobe."

When we were alone, he turned to me. "I know you've got a problem and I'd like to help you." I got that feeling again. *He knows, and he's going to tell everyone.*

"I think you and I need to take the mattress off your bed, hang it over the line behind the building, and send your sheets and blankets to the laundry. We can do that when the other boys go to breakfast this morning and it can stay our secret. Is that okay with you?"

"Yes, sir. That's okay with me."

"Starting tonight, I'm going to wake you up around midnight and take you to the bathroom. We'll see if that doesn't stop this problem. Is that okay with you, Kobe?"

"Yes, sir. That's okay with me."

Nathan and I waited until the last boy left the building. I told Brett that I had to get something and asked him to save a seat at breakfast.

Nathan helped me carry the mattress out. It smelled bad, but Nathan didn't say anything. He gave me a cloth bag and stuffed the sheets, blanket and my PJs into it. He took the bag and told me to go catch up with the other boys.

For the next six weeks, Nathan or some other boy got me up every night at midnight and I went to the bathroom. I wish I could say that was the end of the problem but it wasn't. I had many more accidents, but Nathan and I took care of them just as before. When I prayed at night, I thanked God and my dead mother for Nathan and stopped asking them for help. Like Butch had said, I had learned that those kind of prayers just don't work.

At home, after camp, my problem continued. I continued to wet the bed off and on until junior high school. I would get up early each morning, strip my sheets, take them to the washing machine and then the dryer, and remake my bed, all before I went to school. I became pretty good at doing laundry. At one point, my parents bought a metallic sheet that fit under my regular sheet. When I'd pee, an alarm would go off. It didn't do any good, though. It was supposed to wake me up and stop me from peeing but instead it woke everyone else up and I had to put on clean sheets before they went back to bed. The experiment only lasted a week and then I was back to getting up each morning in a wet bed and washing my sheets.

Most of the kids stayed at camp for two weeks, so twice during the summer, the boys that I had gotten to know would pack up and head home. Several hours later, a new group would arrive and the process of fitting in would start all over. I can't say I ever got good at it – at camp or in the years to follow. Making friends and having friends was never a strong suit for me. Maybe it's because they always seemed to be leaving.

On the third Saturday at camp, Nathan pulled me aside and directed me to the administrative office. "Your mom and dad are here to see you."

I assumed he meant dad and his new wife, Grace Plotner. I ran down the distance and sure enough there was Dad, Grace, and Butch all talking. I was glad to see him. "What are you doing here? I thought you weren't picking us up for another two weeks."

Dad explained that he and Grace were driving to Minnesota to fish for a few weeks and then they'd pick us up on their way home. "Grace and I got married last week in Champaign, and I wanted to bring her by to meet the two of you again."

She looked the same, pretty and nice. "After we pick you up, we will go home to my house on Green Street," she explained. "We have already moved all your things into your new bedrooms."

I didn't know what to think about that, but it seemed to be fine with Butch, so it was fine with me. Besides, with Dad here, maybe he could help straighten out this thing about Cowboy Camp.

"Dad," I started, "they won't let me in Cowboy Camp, and you said that I would be in Cowboy Camp."

"Butch already told me about it, Kobe, and I spoke to the camp administrator. He says it's a rule that you have to be 11-years-old to be in Cowboy Camp because of their insurance."

I didn't know what insurance was, but I wasn't going to leave it at that. "You told me that I would be in Cowboy Camp."

"I made a mistake, but the camp administrator said you could join the boys in Cowboy Camp tomorrow so that you can ride a horse while you're here."

That was enough for me. "I can? Tomorrow? That great!"

We talked some more but all I could think about was getting to ride a horse. They said good-bye and headed off on their honeymoon.

The next day, Billy showed up at Eagles Nest after breakfast to take me to Cowboy Camp to get my horse.

We entered the barn and Billy pointed. "That's Smokey. He's going to be your horse today."

Smokey was the biggest horse I had ever seen. He was light brown with a dark mane and a dark tail. Smokey would do just fine. I felt sure I could handle him.

"All right, let's get him saddled," Billy ordered. "The other boys are ready to leave."

Billy threw a big leather saddle on Smokey's back, tightened the belly straps, put the bridle in Smokey's mouth, and turned to me. "Let me help you up."

I raised my leg to put my foot in the stirrup. Billy boosted me into the saddle, but as I sat down, my foot slipped out of the stirrup. Billy raised the stirrups higher but couldn't get them to match my feet. Outside the barn I could see the other boys waiting on their horses.

"Let's go, Canoe Head. We don't have all day," the Cowboy leader called out.

"Here, put your feet in these straps above the stirrups," Billy told me as he shoved my feet into place and gave me the reins. He slapped Smokey on the rump who then trotted off to join the other horses.

The ride went smoothly. We went down by the lake, up a hill through the woods, and into a meadow. We'd been out about an hour and I felt I was fitting in with the other boys. Then the leader hollered out, "Let 'em run," and the boys and their horses broke into a gentle trot. Smokey took off with them. I wished he would break for the lead. Sure enough, Smokey started to pick up speed and we began to pass the other boys. We were now in a gallop.

I hung on for my life while my butt slapped against the saddle like a shutter in the wind. I tried to push down with my feet but my legs ended well above the stirrups. I dropped one hand from the reins and grabbed the saddle horn. Smokey and I passed the leader like he was standing still.

"Hey, slow him down," the Cowboy leader shouted. "Pull back on the reins. You're going too fast."

I took my hand off the horn and pulled back on the reins with both hands. I gripped Smokey with my legs and tried to hang on. With each stride, my butt slammed down on the saddle and bounced back up. I looked down, opened my hand, and grabbed Smokey's mane. As I looked up, Smokey ran under a tree with a low-hanging branch. Smokey had no trouble making it under the branch, but my forehead was in its direct line.

Whap! The branch hit my head, my grip on Smokey's mane tore loose, and I tumbled over his back. My left foot came free of the straps but my right foot got twisted and my shoulders and head were getting dragged along the ground at Smokey's side. He then made a hard, left turn and my foot came free.

I lay on the ground and heard the other horses approaching. The Cowboy leader arrived first, jumped off his horse, and came to my side. "Are you okay?" he asked as he rolled me over.

I didn't have to answer. My head was bleeding into my eyes and my arms looked like raw hamburger but I was alive and nothing was broken. He and another guy helped me up and got me back to Cowboy Camp.

Back at camp I overheard one of the counselors say, "I guess Smokey smelled the barn and was hungry." A group of counselors, including Billy and the Cowboy leader, later told me that, "If you ever want to be a part of Cowboy Camp and ride horses again, we need to keep this little accident to ourselves. I wouldn't even tell your parents about this."

That sounded logical to me because I didn't think I'd want to ride another horse this week, but I might want to the next time we came to Camp Anachegie "We'll tell Nathan about it," they explained, "and he'll help get your cuts and scrapes taken care of by the nurse. We'll tell her that you fell out of a tree. Okay?"

I nodded my head.

The six weeks ended and Butch and I found ourselves together again outside the administration building waiting to be picked up. Butch asked if I'd had a good time.

Yes, I said. I never told him about my fears and embarrassment and he didn't share with me that he, too, had a bed-wetting problem that summer.

Dad and Grace Plotner picked us up about noon. They'd had a good time and caught a lot of fish. We had a good time at camp. Everybody was happy and we drove home to Champaign.

Butch and Dad knew that I wet the bed every night but no one said anything, no one asked any questions. It was something I experienced alone. Grace Plotner would learn about my problem soon enough and take it upon herself to help me get past it and all the other problems I had accumulated over the past nine years.

# Chapter Eleven
## A New Beginning with a New Mom

We never returned to Patricia Court. Our new home was on Green Street. Grace and her mom, our new Grandma Plotner, lived here. To make room for us, Grandma Plotner moved downtown into an apartment and our new cousin, Judy, moved in with her. Our new home was very different from Patricia Court. Green Street had a white picket fence, trees in the yard, and well-kept grass. Inside, there was big furniture, carpeting, and a separate dining room. Butch and I shared a room that was larger than our old room.

Our mom was gone and everything about her was gone. Her clothes, her hairbrush, even the porcelain figurines that she used to paint. The dollies that she and Grandma Talon used to sew were gone, too. It was as if Kay Talon Grinkmeyer's existence had been erased from Earth, or at least Champaign, Illinois. She, and everything connected with her, had disappeared, and Grace Plotner had filled the void.

We never talked about Mom. We never sat down and looked at old pictures. We never celebrated her birthday or commemorated her passing. We never visited her grave.

We also lost touch with Grandma Talon, who I wouldn't see again for seven years.

Dad explained that Rooney would be joining us in several weeks but we would all be moving again in about six months. "Mom and I are building a new home in Greencroft."

Greencroft didn't mean anything to me at the time, but I would soon learn that it was the country-club neighborhood where the new-rich built homes. Although it was only a mile from Patricia Court, it was a world away economically. I now know that you can sooner change your life with five minutes at the altar than you can with a lifetime's work. I think Dad had come to such a realization.

The first order of business was to buy Butch and me clothes. Grace took us downtown to the store where Grandma Plotner worked and we left with more new clothes then we had old clothes. This new Mom made me feel important and I worked hard to make her like me. In my child's mind, she was Mom now. I had no idea what a stepmother was, but a mom I understood.

This Mom was also a disciplinarian. She had her rules and set out from the start to enforce them. Dinner at Patricia Court had been informal, to say the least. We would be called to eat by the housekeeper, and Butch and I would float in, eat what we wanted, and leave. Dad wasn't there most of the time, and when he was, he didn't seem to care.

Grace ran her house very differently. "If I go to the trouble to fix you dinner, you will show me the courtesy to come to my table with clean hands and face. You will thank the Lord for his blessings, and you will clean your plate."

This took some getting used to, particularly for me. Other than peas and corn, there were few vegetables I liked.

My first introduction to lima beans set the tone for how dinner was conducted in Grace's house.

"Mom, I don't like lima beans," I told her the first night they were served.

"Eat a few, and you may learn to like them," she said.

"But, I ..."

"Do as you mother tells you," Dad stepped in.

I put a small spoonful on my plate but had no intention of eating them.

After several minutes, Grace noticed. "Try your lima beans, Kobe."

I stabbed one lima bean with my fork, painfully lifted it to my mouth, bit into it, scrunched my face, spit it out, and informed the table. "I don't like lima beans."

Grace placed her flatware to the side of her plate and stared at me. After a long pause, she spoke. "You're going to learn how to behave at the table, and you're going to learn to show respect for whoever prepares your meals. You will not leave this table until you clean your plate and that includes your lima beans."

I realized then that spitting out the lima bean was a mistake. I looked to Dad to intervene, but I quickly saw that I was on my own here. I wanted to make my new mom happy but this is where I was going to take a stand. I said nothing and ate everything on my plate except the lima beans.

Butch cleaned his plate. "May I be excused?" he asked, showing he had learned the new phrase required before exiting the table.

"You may," Dad responded.

I caught Dad's eye, and before I could speak, he spoke. "Don't even ask until you clean your plate."

Within ten minutes the table had been cleared, Mom and Dad were in the kitchen, Butch was watching TV, and I remained at the dining room table. It was 6:30.

I knew they wouldn't leave me at the table all night and I was willing to wait them out. Butch and I went to bed at nine on school nights, and they weren't going to force those lima beans down my throat. I would win this battle.

Nine o'clock came and went. I heard Butch say good night and go to bed. Within fifteen minutes Dad came into the dining room and told me to go to bed. I left the table, silently celebrating my victory.

I climbed into bed and Butch asked, "Did you eat them?"

"Nope," I answered in the voice of a victorious warrior. I slept well that night.

The next morning Mom woke Butch and me to get ready for school. We dressed, brushed our teeth, combed our hair, and went into the kitchen for breakfast. I had wet the bed and I had to take care of the sheets first.

Our cereal bowls were in their customary place. Butch's bowl was filled with Cheerios. Mine overflowed with lima beans. More lima beans then I had had on my plate the night before.

Butch dove into his cereal. I sat and contemplated my next move. *"I could go without breakfast."*

"Butch, what would you like for lunch? Peanut butter and jelly or lunch meat?" Mom asked.

Then she turned from the counter where she was making our lunch and gave me the same look I had seen last night. "And what will you be eating for lunch, Kobe?" she asked.

I looked back at her and realized I was out of my league. I dropped my eyes to my cereal bowl, held my breath, and took two bites of lima beans. I swallowed, took a drink of milk, looked back at her and said, "Peanut butter and jelly. please."

She didn't move. She didn't blink. I took two more bites of lima beans and she turned and made my sandwich.

I wouldn't challenge Grace Plotner again for years.

~ ~ ~

A week before Halloween, I told Mom that there was a costume contest at school and I wanted to enter. In the past, Butch and I hadn't dressed up for it. We didn't participate in much of anything at school.

"We'll dress you up and see if you can't win that contest," Mom assured me.

The night before the contest, Mom called me into her room. "I want you to try on your costume tonight so you can be ready tomorrow morning."

Over the next hour, she transformed me from a grubby little boy to a beautiful young lady ready for her junior prom. I wore a seafoam-shaded dress, matched heels, a stuffed bra, a blonde shoulder length wig, earrings, fake eye lashes, and lipstick. I was beautiful. She spent the next hour teaching me to walk in heels and to walk "like a lady." She was having fun and I was making her happy, so I was happy.

The next morning, she put me back in my costume and drove Butch and me to school. She dropped off Butch, who hadn't wanted to participate, and then drove me up to the school door, explaining that she didn't want Butch to be seen with me so that no one would know my identity.

"You can't talk to anyone," she instructed, "or they will recognize your voice. Just shake your head yes or no when anyone speaks to you. This is important because if they can't guess who you are, you can win this contest. Do you want to win?"

"Yeah, I guess so." Having never won anything, I did not really know what she was talking about.

"Kobe, don't you want to be special? Don't you want everyone to envy you? Don't you want everyone to look up to you?"

Again, I didn't understand. I had never thought about anyone considering me special except my dead mom, and now my new mom. And I was no longer sure about my dead mom. But I did know that it was important for Grace to think I was special, so I nodded my head.

"Then you go into that school knowing that you are the prettiest girl there, that you have the best costume, and that you are going to win the Halloween Costume Contest. And do not speak to anyone. Okay?"

I entered my classroom and Mom was right. No one knew who I was and I kept my mouth shut. My teacher picked two of us to enter the contest and she chose me and a classmate. We then joined the other finalists on the playground for the costume parade. All the students and teachers had gathered together as we marched in front of them. With each passing, several students were eliminated and the group got smaller. I could hear the teachers talking among themselves, pointing at me and whispering. Some of them were having more fun than I was. Some were laughing.

I was proud. I was a finalist. Everyone was looking at me and asking, "Who is that pretty girl?"

The only other times people had paid attention to me was when I was in trouble. This was a new feeling, and I liked it. As I made my third pass in front of the teachers, I spotted Mom sitting in her car at the edge of the playground, watching the costume parade. Watching me.

The group of finalists was down to two, a girl in a poodle costume and me, a pretty girl in a prom dress who no one recognized even though she wasn't wearing a mask. Grace Plotner was right. I could be special. I could be a winner.

Mrs. Anderson stepped in front of the poodle and me and said. "And the winner of this year's Halloween Costume Contest is …. Judy Grey as a poodle!"

I didn't care that Judy had won. She did have a neat costume and a lot of work and detail went into it. Then Mrs. Anderson turned to me. "And who are you?"

I looked to the car and I saw Mom clapping. I turned to Mrs. Anderson. "I'm Kobe Grinkmeyer," I said, and lifted off my wig.

All the teachers were watching me. No one was talking to Judy. I felt sorry for her. Technically she had won, yet somehow I felt I had.

I liked that feeling of winning, and with Grace Plotner's help I would learn how to win again and again. Winning and competition would become a driving force throughout my life. Strange as it may seem, this day of cross-dressing was one of those moments that formed my character and influenced how I would turn out in the world.

When Easter arrived the next year, I told Mom that the school had an Easter Bonnet Contest just like the Halloween contest and I wanted to enter.

"Do you have any ideas?" I asked her.

"Let me think about it. We'll come up with something for both you and Butch."

That night she told Butch and me to get our football helmets. They were to be transformed into Easter bonnets.

She cut a hole into the center of a three-foot-by-two-foot cardboard rectangle and slipped a helmet into the hole. "Now put the helmet on," she instructed us. "We're going to wrap the cardboard in the pretty green paper and then we're going to glue Easter eggs, toy rabbits, ducks, and this Easter grass on to the paper. These will be your Easter bonnets."

Butch and I were so proud. We didn't win but we both made the finalists parade, and again Mom was there in her car watching.

~ ~ ~

Butch and I became "participants." We both joined the Boy Scouts. Butch had been a Cub Scout but I never took any interest. But as soon as I was eligible, I asked to join the Boy Scout. I had seen Butch working on projects to become a Second-Class Scout and then a First-Class Scout and I found out there were other levels of achievement all the way up to Eagle Scout. I saw this as a way to compete, a way to stand out.

I joined the Boy Scouts in September 1954 and was awarded my Eagle Scout badge in July 1958. At age 13, I was the youngest boy to have been awarded Eagle in the state of Illinois. This was important to me. I was starting to believe that I could achieve anything I put my mind to. Dad had told me, "Take the word 'can't' out of your vocabulary. You can do anything you believe you can do, but you have to believe in yourself. If you don't believe in yourself, how can you expect anyone else to believe in you?"

Mom, Dad, and I were invited to the stage at Westview Elementary School where I would receive my Eagle Scout badge. The auditorium was full of other scouts and their parents. There was even a reporter and photographer from the Champaign newspaper. Mom was pregnant and was due in less than a month. The doctor had suggested she not attend, but she told him she had to. She received a necklace with a small eagle on it, honoring her for all the help she had given me. The awards were presented by Warren Smith, the regional scouting director.

~ ~ ~

In January 1956 we moved to Greencroft. This was not a normal house, certainly nothing like where I had ever lived. It was built in the style of the fifties, constructed of redwood siding and glass – a lot of glass. Its most outstanding feature was its butterfly roof. This was Chuck and Grace making a statement: We've arrived. They were members of the Champaign Country Club. Their new home was featured in the *Champaign Times* Sunday Home section. Grace was driving a new pink, black, and white Buick Roadmaster.

Grace had visited the Chicago Furniture Mart to purchase new furniture, much of it made by the most celebrated designers in the country. The house had Eames chairs, a Noguchi table, and a Starburst clock. My brothers and I now know that if we could put our hands on some of those furnishings today, they'd be worth tens of thousands of dollars.

Butch, Rooney, and I each had our own living spaces, although they would be called cubicles today. We shared one large room divided into three separate quarters, each containing a bed, a built-in desk, a dresser, and a closet. We each had a bamboo curtain that we could pull across the entrance, separating us from the common area.

The house had three levels. You entered at ground level through the carport. The first level contained the living room, dining room, Dad's office, and the kitchen. At the right side of our home we had a two-story section. The upper level had the master bedroom, our bedrooms, and a bathroom. The lower level had a rec-room, bath, and utility room. The lower level was about two-thirds underground. Dad's friend, an architect, called it a tri-level.

The family living center was the rec-room where the built-in TV, Dad's bar, and a game table was located. There was even a shuffleboard game laid into the vinyl tile floor. We had come a long way from Patricia Court.

Spring in Illinois brought rain. One Sunday morning, the house awoke to the sound of Rooney's gleeful voice. "Mom! Dad! Come see the rec room. It's a swimming pool and there are Baby Ruth candy bars floating in it."

Butch and I beat Mom and Dad to confirm Rooney's observation. There was four feet of water in our rec-room.

"Rooney, those aren't Baby Ruth candy bars," Butch said. "Those are turds."

"Mom! Dad! We have turds in our swimming pool," Rooney amended his earlier proclamation.

We soon found out why. Our house was on a corner, which meant that the main sewer line ran down the side of our lot. Dad's friend, the proud architect, had connected our home directly into the sewer, so when it filled with rainwater and rose to the level of our hook-up, our neighbor's sewage backed up and filled our rec-room. It turned out that this was within standard building code, and ours wasn't the only home subject to turd pools when it rained.

We spent the rest of the day waiting for the rain to stop. Mom and Dad went to the hardware store and purchased rubber gloves, coal shovels, mops, and lots of bleach. Before they left, we were told, "Don't leave the house. Don't answer the phone. And never tell anyone about this."

At about four o'clock the rain stopped and by five the pool started to empty. By eight, the water level was low enough that Mom, Dad, Butch, and I started pushing the water toward the floor drain. Grandma Plotner had been called in to look after Rooney. Dad used the coal shovel to gather up the turds, toilet paper, some small balloons he wouldn't discuss, and other objects found in the raw sewage.

The furniture was carried out to the patio and hosed down, and then Mom started pouring out bleach to disinfect everything. We finished about 1 a.m. Our final instructions before going to bed were again, "Don't you ever tell anyone about this." Mom and Dad were already thinking about selling the house.

The turd swimming pool appeared two more times before a solution was found. Several years later, he and the architect were pheasant hunting together when his "friend" took a load of buckshot in the ass. For years, Dad claimed it was an accident.

Our solution to holding off the sewage was the "key," a ten-foot steel pole that came to a "T" on one end and had a three-inch socket wrench head on the other. A plumber had installed a shut-off valve in our sewer line in our front yard. Whenever it started to rain hard, Butch or I would grab the key, run out in the rain, remove a small cover, slide the key down a pipe, and turn the key to shut off our sewer connection. The only problem was that the hole for the key was in the middle of the front yard, in full view of the neighbors. It was decided that the task of closing off the sewer line had to be done under cover of darkness whenever possible.

Mom and Dad would watch the evening news to determine if the valve needed to be shut off. If the weatherman predicted heavy rain, Butch and I would move into action. If headlights appeared from any direction, we would run into the carport, leaving the key protruding from the ground. We'd stay hidden until the car passed and then return to finish the job.

With the sewage line shut off, we couldn't flush toilets or run any water in the house. We had two toilets and it could rain for days in Illinois. Whenever the danger passed, Butch and I would run out to the sewer access on the street, stick our head into the opening, and look down to see if the water level had receded below our tap line. Once it did, we got the key and reversed the process, preferably in the dark.

Not being able to flush the toilets or tell anyone about our problem meant that you pooped into the toilet but didn't flush. After a while, you would end up pooping on top of other peoples' poop. When it got close to your ass, it really stunk. In the fifties there weren't shopping malls on every corner so public restrooms were not an option. We just learned to live with our problem because no one wanted another clean-up. I still have nightmares of going to the toilet and finding it full of poop and toilet paper, gagging on the stink, and deciding to "hold it." That was the phrase. "Can't you just hold it? It will stop raining soon."

Summer in Illinois brought wind. The front of the house presented an "L" with the carport as the leg of the "L." The carport face was a beautiful sandstone wall, and the weight of the roof was supported by three steel posts.

Our family was having dinner in the kitchen one windy evening when we were startled by a loud thud and a jarring of the house. We ran to the front door and saw that the stone wall had collapsed into the front yard due to air pressure in the carport. There it lay in perfect shape, not a mortar joint broken, not a stone out of place.

The whole incident was so bizarre it was funny. We were all laughing. "What if . . ." Mom said through giggles, "what if it rains? What if it rains hard?"

Dad explained. "Boys, the key is under the wall."

The winter brought snow and cold in Illinois. Our neighborhood had been built in the middle of a corn field. There were no trees and no hills, so when the snow came, it drifted up against the house. The big glass windows iced up and Mom had to put towels at the base to catch the melting water. The walls on the staircase would frost up from the cold wind blowing through the siding.

We lived at 71 Greencroft for six years, and every season presented a new challenge. When we moved, we left the key but offered no explanation to the new owners.

# Chapter Twelve

## Kobe, You're Dumb – Get Used to It

My life had taken an unmistakable new direction. Grace had not only brought money into our lives, but she established discipline, order, and pride. These concepts were new to me, but I liked the change.

And yet, Champaign – and the country – was full of fear. People in our neighborhood were building bomb shelters in their back yards in preparation for a Russian invasion. I remember seeing an airplane fly overhead and worrying that it could be a Soviet bomber. At school, we had air raid drills signaled by the blasting of a horn in the hallway. We would crawl under our desks until the drill was over.

I continued to have problems in school. I was at least two grade-levels behind in reading, I couldn't spell, and math was beyond my comprehension. Yet I excelled in Boy Scouts. I was good in sports. And I was becoming a good kid.

Every Thursday in fifth grade, Mrs. Reynolds made students stand in front of the class and practice that week's spelling words. One day I was doing fine until she came to me.

"Kobe, spell *second*."

I thought, sounded it out, and spelled, "S E C O U N D."

"No," she said, "try again."

"S E C K O U N D."

"No, come to the front of the class and sound it out and try again."

I started to get hot, my hands were sweating, and I felt sick. I walked to the front of the class and faced my friends and classmates. I took a deep breath.

Mrs. Reynolds repeated her instructions. "Kobe, spell *second* for the class."

"S E C O U N D."

"No, that's what you gave me the first time. Try again."

In the back of the class, Jay Smith laughed. Jay was a friend. We played baseball together. He was helping me become a better batter.

"Try again, Kobe" Mrs. Reynolds repeated. "Spell *second*."

I didn't even think. I blurted out, "S E C O U N D."

Jay laughed harder. He slapped his leg, he was laughing so hard.

I started to cry. I was in fifth grade standing in front of my classmates, unable to spell second, and I was crying. Since that moment in the hospital, the last time I saw my mother alive, I had vowed never to cry again. Somehow through the loneliness, and the fear of humiliation, I had managed to hold my tears through six long weeks of summer camp. But here, in this classroom, in front of my friends, I couldn't hold them back. They stung as the streamed down my face.

"Sit down, Kobe. Class, how do you spell second?"

Their answer was deafening.

"S! E! C! O! N! D!"

I sunk into my chair, trying to pull myself together. "You're not like them," I said to myself. "You're dumb. You're the dumbest kid in this school and everyone knows it."

After lunch I went out to the playground. Jay Smith was standing with a group of boys. I pushed my way through until we were face to face and I punched him in the nose. Hard. He fell to the ground, grasping at his face. "What was that for?" he shouted.

"You know what that was for, Jay," I replied, and walked away.

Two years earlier, I would have been on top of him, fists flying. Someone would have had to pull me off. Jay might not have realized it, but I had come a long way.

At home that evening, I told Mom what had happened. She took me in her arms. "We can't let that happen again." I knew she didn't mean me hitting other boys. Both she and Dad had taught us to stand up for ourselves, to not back away from defending yourself or your honor.

Mom adopted the role of personal tutor. We would sit at the kitchen table and she would drill me on my spelling words every week. Every night she would help Butch and me with our homework. She helped us memorize multiplication tables. She would even read books to us so that we could write a book report. I don't know if I got a lot better, but thanks to her, I did get by.

# Chapter Thirteen

## You're not the Meanest Dog in the Park

In September 1956, I entered the sixth grade. Butch, a year ahead of me, hadn't done well in class and it was decided that he would repeat sixth grade. Butch had been angry ever since Mom died and school came hard for him – even harder than it was for me. Often, he vented his anger on me. I could easily set him off. We usually came to blows, and I would get the worst of it. That didn't stop me from irritating him every chance I got. Yet he was my best friend.

Because of the Baby Boom, Westview wasn't able to accommodate all students. Butch and I were among a group of sixth graders assigned to Edison Junior High, which was downtown. We would have to take a school bus and there would be new kids in our class.

Edison Junior High was the old high school, a four-story building that each day received half of Champaign's seventh through ninth graders. Our sixth-grade class met in the southeast corner room on the fourth floor. There were thirty-two kids in my class, and I knew four of them from Westview. There were Negro boys and girls, which we hadn't had at our school. There were hoods with long, greasy hair and leather coats. They smoked cigarettes before school and one of them arrived on the back of his brother's motorcycle. His name was Donald Day.

The first several days were all about getting acquainted: acquainted with each other, the school, the teacher, and our position in our new surroundings. Each of us had a history and reputation from our former schools and they were quickly communicated. The smart kids established their position as did the jokers, the tough guys and girls, and the teacher suck-ups.

This was also the time when boys and girls started noticing each other. I had taken an interest in one of the girls on the school bus, and she liked me. I would make a point to sit with her or near her every day on the bus. Sharon was my girlfriend in the innocent sense of the word. One day after lunch, Sharon and I were talking when Donald Day walked up to us. He ignored me and spoke to Sharon. "I'd like to kiss you and your tits."

I hadn't kissed Sharon, and I certainly hadn't thought about kissing her tits. Sharon was embarrassed as well as scared. This was Donald Day, after all. I had to defend her honor. I pushed Donald Day with both hands. "Get out of here and leave us alone."

Donald recoiled with a right cross to the left side of my head. I fell and he was on top of me, pinning my arms to the ground with his knees and bending over into my face. The cross he wore around his neck was slapping my chin. He reached into his leather jacket and pulled out a switchblade. Click. The point of the knife was now at my neck. His hot breath rushed over my face. "I'm not interested in your little girlfriend. I want you to know who I am, and who you are. Do you understand?"

I looked into Donald Day's eyes and knew he had been here before. I recognized that this stand was more important to him then it was to me and that I was no match for him.

"I understand."

Donald got up, walked away, and we never had another problem.

The summer between sixth and seventh grade, Donald Day and his older brother were arrested for a gas station robbery. Donald's brother had shot a man during the crime. I never saw Donald Day again.

But he had taught me an important lesson that day in the school yard: There are some people (and organizations) you don't want to take on for any reason. I haven't always adhered to that lesson, though. I have stood up for principle, honor, and what I thought was right, even when facing a stronger adversary. Sometimes I prevailed, but more often I have suffered.

# Chapter Fourteen
## I Am Capable of Evil

Our class clown was Kenny Forest. He lived just a few blocks from us but I didn't get to know him until sixth grade. Kenny knew no boundaries. He would do anything and worry about the consequences later. He quickly drew Butch and me into his schemes.

Halloween that year had little to do with traditional trick-or-treating. It was Kenny's opportunity for the ultimate trick. The week before Halloween, he took an old pair of blue jeans and sewed a heavy shirt to the waistband. He sewed the arm and leg holes shut and then stuffed his mannequin with newspaper. He stitched a cloth bag to the shirt for a head and topped it with a ball cap. Kenny, Butch, Danny Owens, and I carried our "little brother" with us as we went from house to house. At about eight o'clock Kenny pulled two twenty-foot pieces of rope out of his candy bag and tied one length to each of "little brother's" arms.

"Come with me," he said. "This will be fun."

We walked to a lightly traveled road behind the school where new houses were being built, which meant there were no streetlights. Kenny laid the mannequin on the side of the road and carried one end of the rope into the ditch, where he and

Danny took cover. Butch and I were assigned to the ditch on the other side.

"When a car comes down the road," Kenny instructed, "I'll pull the rope hard while you hold your end loose. But hold it high so 'little brother' looks like he's running across the road. 'Little brother' will fly in front of the car and the car will hit him. We'll stay in the ditch until the driver gets out and then we'll grab him and run."

Kenny's idea sounded like a lot of fun. We waited for several minutes until headlights approached. When the car was almost even with us, Kenny yelled, "Now!" I stood up and held my end of the rope high, letting it slip through my hand as the car's front fender slammed into "little brother" with a thud. I dove into the ditch.

The car screeched to a stop. An elderly lady opened the car door and ran out to see what she had hit. I was no more than eight feet away from her. The interior light illuminated her face and I could see horror in her eyes. If she had looked to the ditch, our eyes would have met. She ran toward the body in the road and I could hear her saying, "Are you all right? I'm so sorry. I didn't see you." There was terror in her voice. She was about to cry.

Just before she reached the mannequin, we all sprang out of the ditch and ran within three feet of her, snagging "little brother" and bolting into the darkness.

Her voice changed to rage and anger. "Damn you little son-of-a-bitches! You almost gave me a heart attack."

Hearing the lady call me a "son-of-a-bitch" made me stop in my tracks. Butch came back, grabbed my arm, and pulled me away.

We got better with each of the next three cars as Kenny's timing improved. I was always within eight feet of the driver as they exited their car. I would see their face fully lit, full of terror. Each driver stopped and hurried to aid what they thought was a child lying in the middle of the road. In one case, the car's wheels ran over "little brother." Each time we would spring from the ditches, grab our toy, and quickly slip into the night.

The next time two headlights approached; I could see it was a pick-up truck. Butch manned the rope this time. "Now!" Kenny screamed and "little brother" sprinted across the street right in front of the pick-up. The trucks lights illuminated what looked like an 11-year-old boy – I did not have this view when I was handling the rope.

After the pickup hit our brother, the driver slammed on his brakes and the tires screamed. The door swung open before the truck had come to a complete stop and I saw a man in his 30s in blue jeans. Just as his alligator-skinned cowboy boot hit the pavement, he saw me.

I jumped out of the ditch and ran, but within four strides the man had caught up with me. He grabbed my arm and spun me around, pulling me to his face. "You little bastard," he growled. "I'll give you a trick you'll remember."

Out of the corner of my eye I saw Butch running past. He was pulling 'little brother's" rope with him. It caught the man about ankle high and pulled his legs out from under him, knocking him down so he hit the pavement hard on his butt. This freed me from his grip and I took off, faster than I had ever run in my life.

Within seconds he was chasing after me. I darted up a narrow board that led into a house under construction. I ran through the house, jumped out the back door, and took off across the backyard. The man was not as sure-footed on the board as I had been which allowed me to put some distance between us.

Once he cleared the house, he started to gain on me, so I dove into a ditch, probably a septic tank field line, and laid still. There was no light other than the moon, and it wasn't that bright. He was within five feet of my hiding place and I could hear him breathing heavily. He wandered off to the next house and his heavy boots pounded on the plywood floors. As he started to return to his truck, he shouted, "You little bastard. I saw your face. I'll hunt you down. I'll find you." Then he drove away, his tires squealing.

Butch, Kenny, and Danny had watched the whole thing from their hiding place on top of a mound of dirt fifty feet away. They came and pulled me out of the trench that had saved me. Within two minutes, they had me laughing about the whole nightmare and we headed back to the street in search of our next victim.

Our evil trick ended with the arrival of a police car. The man in the alligator boots had been true to his threat. Lucky for us, we spotted the police before they spotted us. Kenny tucked "little brother" under his arm and the four us ran home laughing and reliving our adventure all the way there.

Looking back on my life, that night's high jinx represent the meanest act I have ever committed. I don't know what happened to Kenny Forest. I'm happy now to say that we grew apart and ran with different crowds in the following years.

~ ~ ~

# Chapter Fifteen
## Mom Is Having a Baby

It had been almost four years since Dad remarried and formed our new family. Mom had taken control and Butch and I had been turned around. Discipline, direction, and respect for ourselves and others had been introduced into our lives. We were far from perfect – our scholastic achievements still fell short – but we were trying.

It must have been decided in January that Mom would try to have a child. She was thirty-eight years old so it was now or never. This was not a topic of conversation at the dinner table; Butch, Rooney, and I learned the news in late February.

"Rooney, you're going to have a little brother," Grandma Plotner told us.

I was happy for Mom and understood why she would want to have her own child. It was a big task joining our family after the death of our mom and raising three boys not her own.

One afternoon I told her I wanted to attend one of the bi-weekly YMCA Friday night dances. To my surprise, she was glad I wanted to dance. Mom and Dad went out every Saturday night for dinner at the Moose Lodge or country club and I knew she liked to dance. I figured she must be a good at it.

"If you're going to a dance, you'll need to know how," she said. "I'll teach you."

She took me into the living room, an area normally off limits All the good furniture was here and there was no reason for us boys to be on it. She opened a door on our teak breakfront – one of the Chicago purchases – and revealed a record player and some albums. I didn't know we had a record player, but then why would I?

Mom stood five foot nine and weighed about 135 pounds. She was shapely and filled out a bathing suit quite well. She knew it and was proud. I think you would call her a "sexual woman," a phrase I learned from Chuck Hunter who lived down the street. She put on a Dean Martin song, rocked back and forth to get the beat, and stepped into me. She took my right hand and put it on her back, held my left hand out and up, and started moving with the music.

I stumbled around the room watching my feet, trying not to step on her toes.

"No, no… look at me," she told me with a big smile on her face, obviously having fun. "Just move with me. Let me lead." She pulled me in tight to her body.

"Put your right foot between my feet and let your legs flow with mine. You need to feel every move I make and move with me." She continued humming with the music.

I felt uncomfortable but soon realized that she wasn't, and I knew this was how I was going to learn to dance. She was as serious about making me a good dancer as she was about anything else she had taught me. Within a half hour, I was moving with her and I felt ready for the Friday night dance.

"I think I've got it."

"Not yet," she said. "I'm doing all the leading and you're following me. You have to learn to lead. The man always leads."

"Oh?" I didn't quite understand.

"We'll work on that tomorrow. I have to make dinner now." She turned off the music and escorted me out of the living room. "Go work on your spelling. I'll test you after dinner."

I'm going to best the best dancer next Friday night, I thought as I climbed the steps to my room. All the girls will want to dance with me.

"We'll work on fast dancing after you learn to lead," she hollered after me.

"Fast dancing?" Once again, I didn't understand.

The dance lessons continued through the week. Butch would have nothing to do with it. He wasn't going to dance with Mom, and that was okay with me. I was enjoying it. After dinner on Thursday night, Mom called out to Dad. "Kobe and I have something to show you."

She grabbed my hand and I went willingly and confidently. In no time we were dancing around the living room. "Isn't he good? I think he's a natural," she announced.

"Can I see you and Dad dance?" I asked.

They were only too glad to oblige. I could see that when Mom and Dad got on the dance floor, others moved to the side. They danced through the house – where Dad went, Mom followed. They twirled. He dipped her and she kicked up her leg. At the end of the song, she spun on one foot. They looked like professionals, and she was my teacher.

Butch had never accepted the change in moms as readily as I did. He sometimes resented that I had let Grace in so easily and forgotten our first mother so quickly. He was angry and showed it.

But it wasn't that I forgotten her. I wasn't at peace. Not at all. I just wasn't willing to face it. I didn't know how to deal my feelings, so I buried them and everything connected with them. I wasn't sure about my first Mom's love, God's love, Jesus's love, or the Virgin Mary's love. And who would I talk to about that empty feeling inside me? So I chose to move on and make the best of what I had.

Butch continued to direct his anger toward me. It seemed that any little thing I did could unleash his fury. I started to hear "I'm going to kill you" again, but it didn't really bother me. I knew he wouldn't kill me. He might hurt me bad but he wasn't going to kill me.

Mom wasn't as tolerant. "Butch, you've got to stop saying that to Kobe or anyone else. Do you understand me?"

"Yes, ma'am," he answered.

"I'm going to kill you," he told tell me the next day.

"That's it. I told you to stop that, and I meant it," Mom said as she stormed into our room. "You both are coming with me Saturday morning. Be ready to leave the house at 7 a.m."

That Saturday we pulled out of the driveway at seven on the dot. I took the front seat; Butch sat in the back by himself. We stopped in front of Holy Cross Catholic Church. Mom climbed the steps and opened the huge wood door. She stepped aside and directed us both in. "Go to the front of the church."

Our footsteps echoed through the empty sanctuary. We stopped at the front, standing next to each other. Mom was two steps behind.

"Butch, you're going to spend the entire day here in church. I want you to talk to God and find a way to overcome that anger inside you. Here's your lunch. I'm sure there's a bathroom somewhere. I'll be back to pick you up at six o'clock." She handed him a brown paper bag.

"Kobe, you come with me. We're going to go and have some fun." I followed her to the back of the church, her high heels clacking on the marble floor.

When we reached the car, she turned to me. "I've got to do some shopping. We'll go out to lunch and do whatever you want to do. The important thing is that when Butch asks you what we did, make it sound like it was great. We have to break him of this."

Over lunch, I got up the nerve to ask Mom a question I had wondered about for years.

"Did you know about Rooney when you got married?"

"Know what about Rooney?"

"Did you know that he existed? Did you know that there were three of us?"

She laughed. "Sure, I did. I met him when Dad introduced me to his family in Cincinnati."

"Oh, I thought that maybe…"

She interrupted me before I could go on.

"But there is something that your father did. If I had known it, I wouldn't have married him." She went back to eating her sandwich, staring off to a far-away place.

When I thought she had come back, I asked, "What did he do?"

She looked at me, squeezed her eyes tight, then opened them and looked away. "No… that's not for me to tell, not now anyway. He's your dad."

"What?"

"I said no."

There was a long pause and then we started talking about something else.

Butch didn't stop threatening to kill me, but Mom never heard it again. In fact, I think Butch and Mom started to get closer.

The pregnancy wasn't easy for her. Aside from her age, she had complications with blood pressure. She couldn't put on excess weight. Every afternoon for six months she and Butch would get on my bike and go for a half-hour ride. At first it was funny to see her riding my English bike not knowing how to shift the gears and just use the hand brakes. It got even funnier as her belly grew, but she continued to ride every day, rain or shine, until the day she went to the hospital.

We were hoping for a little sister but it wasn't to be. Steve came home ten days after his birth on August 18, 1958.

What happened next caught us all by surprise, especially Butch, Rooney, and me.

# Chapter Sixteen

## Welcome Home – Your Boys, My Son

S teve was cute, clearly more a Plotner then a Grinkmeyer. His hair was black like the Plotners, not blond like his brothers. His features were long and narrow like the Plotners, not short and broad like ours.

Grandma Plotner had a new toy, her baby boy. Rooney was the first to notice the change. There were no more sleepovers at Grandma Plotner's. The new clothes stopped coming. Everything now was for Steve.

Maybe it was that we were entering our teens, but suddenly Butch and I started hearing that we had become disrespectful of Mom, reported to Dad nearly every evening. What used to be an acceptable response to a question or request became "talking back."

"Go brush your teeth."

"I will after I eat breakfast."

"Don't you talk back to me. When I tell you to do something, you do it. You don't talk back to me. Your father will hear about this."

We became "your boys" or "Chuck's boys." Butch and I quickly realized that what had been was no more. The belt entered our lives. "Wait until your father gets home. He'll take care of the two of you."

Whippings became a regular part of Dad's return from a week on the road. In the beginning we'd scream out in pain, but as they continued, they felt less severe and we started biting our lip to not give Dad the satisfaction. The strategy didn't work.

"You boys better scream when I hit you with the belt or she'll demand that I whip you again," he confessed one day. "So let's work together. I don't like this anymore then you do."

So we gave Mom what she wanted. Screams from hell. It became a contest between Butch and me as to who could scream the loudest and longest: "Ahhhhhhh….ahhhhhhhh……ahhhhhhhh!!"

Mom no longer had time to help with homework. Steve took all her attention. When I asked Dad to help me with a writing assignment, he said, "Sure I'll have time tomorrow afternoon." The next afternoon, I went into his office. "Can you help me with that writing assignment?"

He shuffled some papers and handed me three handwritten pages. "Copy this and turn it in. I did it for you."

I went to my room and copied it word for word into my assignment book. The story was about two boys who build a rocket in their backyard and fly it to the moon to prove to the world it was made of cheese. I loved it. It was original. It was funny. And it was about boys my age. I was sure that the teacher would love it, too. The next day I turned it in.

Two days later I got my assignment book back and opened it up expecting to see an A which would bring my grade average up, something I desperately needed. Instead, I found an F. Next to it was a note written in red: "I don't know who wrote this, but I do know who didn't."

The next week Dad asked, "Did you get your assignment back yet?"

"I got it back last Friday."

"How did we do?"

"I got an… F. My teacher knew I didn't write it."

"Oh," was all he said.

~ ~ ~

Butch and I were pulling weeds in the flower bed. Every evening we had to do a chore before dinner before we could visit with our friends. This was the hour when something would always happen to get us in trouble with Mom. Today we decided to keep our heads down, do as we were told, and keep our mouths shut.

"What has happened around here?" I asked Butch. "I can't seem to do anything right anymore. What's with Mom?"

"Mom and Grandma Plotner got what they wanted," he said.

"What do you mean?"

"Mom loves Steve so much that she's afraid if she loves anyone else, Steve will be starved for love. The Plotners are incapable of loving anyone other than their own."

"What?"

"Look at her brother, Uncle Wilber. Is he a loving man? Does he seem warm or cold to you?"

"Cold, I guess."

"Look at how Grandma Plotner dropped Rooney. She doesn't want anything to do with him anymore. You watch. Dad's up next and our lives will go back to where we were, on our own. Get prepared. little brother. You're about to become Kobe Nobody."

"Where are you getting all this?"

"I've been talking to a counselor at school. Have been since they held me back in sixth grade."

"Okay, the part about Rooney, you, and me I can see. But Steve is Dad's son as much as he's Mom's."

"She's got what she wanted from him. Their marriage started to fall apart when she put two and two together and discovered that he was dating her while Mom was dying in the hospital."

"I don't believe that," I said. But inside I knew it was true. That was the secret she wouldn't tell me that Saturday when we had left Butch at the church.

"Mom didn't believe it either until Grandma Plotner went down to the courthouse and produced our mother's death certificate."

"How do you know all this?" I asked.

"She told me all about it one day when we were riding bikes. She's got what she wanted from Dad now."

"What do we do?"

"What can we do? Just stay out of the way. What's going to happen is going to happen, and there's nothing we can do about it."

Once we finished weeding and got our work inspected by Mom, we were free until dinner. Butch went over to Kenny Forest's house to see what he was cooking up, and I took a walk.

I liked to cross Kirby Avenue and wander around the new houses to see what the carpenters, bricklayers, and plumbers were doing. But this day I went behind the new homes and stepped into the corn field. Butch and I had worked for the

University of Illinois last year on a de-tasseling crew, gathering pollen on a research farm. The work was dirty, hard, and hot. The corn leaves cut your arms, so we only lasted one week. But I learned to like the peace I found in a corn field.

I walked down the rows and listened to the wind blowing through the stalks. I could see cars heading down Kirby but they couldn't see me. An airplane flew over but I felt sure the people in the plane couldn't see me either. I felt safe and alone. The rows were clean, devoid of weeds.

I came here to think – about what Butch had told me and about how things were changing. Mom had Steve now and wouldn't be interested in me like she had been. I had felt it happening but Butch actually said it.

I hadn't known about Dad dating Mom before our first mom had died. Why would he have done that? Had he stopped loving Mom when she got sick, or when we moved from St. Bernard? Can people stop loving other people so fast? What is love, anyway? Did Mom love me when she died? Did our new mom ever love me? Can you only love so many people at one time?

Will anyone ever love me, forever?

I laid down in one of the rows, looked up into the sky, and tried to answer all my questions. My mind just flooded with more.

Does this God, if there is one, really know what's going to happen before it happens? And if there is and he does, why is he letting these things happen to me? If Mom's soul went to heaven and she's with this God, why is *she* letting these things happen to me?

Is this all my fault?

I had a lot of questions but I wasn't finding answers. I put my hands behind my head and looked up into the sky. It was clean blue with few clouds. There was nothing between me and God and Mom.

Suddenly, a grasshopper jumped onto my chest. I lay still, leaving my hands behind my head. The grasshopper didn't know what I was. It turned and looked at me, then turned again and hopped onto a corn stalk. I watched it hang there as those big eyes seemed to look back at me. I felt sure it knew I was there. Neither of us moved for what seemed like a long time. In that moment, we both felt safe.

I walked out of the corn field not knowing any more than I did before I went in, except for one thing.

"We are," I was convinced, "on our own."

# Chapter Seventeen
## Who Decides if You're Good Enough?

I had played backyard football since Patricia Court and I knew this was the sport for me. I had everything it would take to be an outstanding running back: speed, no fear of hitting other people, and my dad had played fullback in high school. This would be my opportunity to excel. I wouldn't be a Bluebird at football.

Champaign High School had a ninth-grade football team and tryouts were held in the practice field. Potential players were told to appear in gym shoes, gym shorts, and a T-shirt. Sixty-five prospects showed up for tryouts. Thirty-six boys would be chosen for the team.

The freshman team had two coaches: Mr. Klitzing coached the backs and receivers. Mr. Hornaday coached the lineman.

Mr. Hornaday was a big man, in good shape, with acne scars on his face. He had a crew cut and big, strong legs. I figured I would look like him when I reached his age, particularly the acne scars. But he was the line coach and I was a running back, so I'd have to get to know him later.

I trotted over with two-thirds of the boys to report to Mr. Klitzing. He was also the head wrestling coach; assistant freshman football coach was just a fill-in for him. He was a small wiry man with a big voice. It will be easy to impress him, I thought.

Mr. Klitzing explained the procedure. "I'm going to put you boys through a series of exercises to determine which of you belong over with Mr. Hornaday and which of you I'll keep on the team as running backs and receivers. There are four running back positions and two receiver positions. I'm going to keep eighteen of you."

I looked at my competition, and even though I was smaller than most of them – I weighed about 125 pounds – I figured I would be fine because of my speed and I knew my capabilities.

"The first thing we're going to do is run the 25-yard dash," he instructed. "I want three of you to run at a time. If I call out your lane number, come over and give me your name."

I positioned myself in the third group to run on the inside lane. When we stepped up to the line, Mr. Klitzing shouted out," Take your marks, get set, go!"

I got a good start and easily beat my two competitors. "Lane number one and lane number two. Your names?"

"Kobe Grinkmeyer," I said. Bob Evans gave his name too. He was about three inches taller than me and trying out for receiver.

I felt good about my performance. From gym class I knew I was one of the fastest boys in ninth grade. The only kid who consistently beat me was Willie Clark, a Negro boy, who wasn't trying out.

Mr. Klitzing called out the names he had accumulated from the first races and asked us to run again. Again, I won my heat.

"Next, you're going to hit the blocking sled, two at a time from a three-point stance. This is a three-point stance," he said, crouching down. "Let me see each of you take this position."

I got into line with classmate Terry Fairbanks on my right. He had several inches and twenty pounds on me, so when we hit the sled together, it veered slightly to his side.

"Fairbanks, stand over there," Mr. Klitzing said. This division of the group continued throughout the sled drill. Those of us who weren't selected were asked to hit the sled one more time. A few more joined the group standing to the side.

"OK, over to the tires. We're going to run the tires."

The tires were over by the fence that bordered the practice field. I was surprised to see Dad standing outside it. He motioned for me over. "After you run the tires, go join the group over there whether or not Mr. Klitzing tells you to," he said.

"Dad, I can't do that."

"Kobe, Mr. Klitzing thinks you're too small to play football, and he's not going to choose you. You need to choose yourself."

"He'll choose me this time," I said, cutting off our conversation so I could run back to the group.

I got in line and ran the tires. Mr. Klitzing didn't call me out.

"Now for the agility drill," Mr. Klitzing announced. He turned his back and moved toward the track. I counted twelve boys in the selected group. I ran over and stood between Bob Evans and Butch, my brother. I looked over to Dad and he smiled.

I was on the team. I would go on to make the all-county and all-state teams four years later.

I learned two things that day: One, if you always follow the rules, you will limit your possibilities. And two, your superiors don't always know best.

# Chapter Eighteen
## Fear: You Can Have It or You Can Dish It

Two days after making the freshman football team I was feeling pretty good about myself. I was standing in the lunch line waiting to pick up my tray when a Negro boy named Bill Sidney walked up and cut into line in front of some white boys. "Step out of my way, I'm in front of you," he said.

He didn't go to the front of the line and cut in there. He was purposely challenging as many people as he could by starting farther back and cutting into and out of the line while moving toward the front. I watched him cut in front of Terry Fairbanks, who just stepped back and let Bill in. Terry was a big boy. At five foot ten and 145 pounds, he was one of the biggest in our class. Bill Sidney was about five foot five and solid but no match for Terry. Yet Terry backed down. I couldn't believe what I was seeing. Bill proceeded to belittle Terry and then turned to move farther up the line.

As he moved right past me toward his next victim, I grabbed his arm and turned him toward me. I clinched my fist and cocked my arm. "The line starts behind me."

"What did you say?"

"The line starts behind me." I didn't look him in the eye. Instead, I concentrated on his nose. If he made the wrong move, that was where my fist would make contact. *Swing through your target*, I told myself, tightening my body into a coiled spring.

Bill Sidney had bullied his way all the way through school to eighth grade. I don't imagine he had been challenged in years, certainly not by a smaller white boy. He asked again: "What did you say to me?"

"You heard me."

"I wasn't hungry anyway," he muttered as he walked away and out of the lunchroom.

One week later my friends and I were sitting at a long table eating our lunch when Bill Sidney approached us. Terry Fairbanks was about three seats down from me on the other side of the table. Bill sat down next to Terry, pushing another student aside. Everyone stopped talking. Terry had fear in his eyes.

"Hey, Terry. Do you like Payday candy bars?" Bill asked.

"Yeah," Terry replied, his voice trembling.

Bill unzipped his fly, reached into his pants, and took out an unwrapped Payday candy bar. "Here. I've been keeping this next to my dick all day for you." He handed Terry the candy bar. "Eat it. All of it."

Terry took it. As he chewed, Bill moved his eyes to meet mine. He had established a new ground that he controlled in my world. He might not challenge me directly, but he was willing to challenge my friends. And I let him. I figured Terry Fairbanks should be able to take care of himself.

# Chapter Nineteen
## You Tried to Kill My Baby!

At Edison Junior High School, it was the custom that on the first Friday of May, a handful of students would assume the roles of principal, vice principal, and other administrative posts. The positions were filled with an election held by the eighth-grade class. Bob Evans was selected as principal, Sherry Smith was vice principal, and Butch Forsyth was to be school secretary.

By now my brother Butch and I were established in the group of popular kids. I'm not quite sure how we made the cut, but we were happy to be included.

Looking back, I suspect most of our classmates thought we came from a wealthy family. Greencroft, where we lived, was a new development with big homes. My parents belonged to the country club and went out to fancy restaurants. Butch and I continued to caddy at the country club and sometimes got to use the country club pool. Of course, none of this was possible before Dad married Mom but they didn't know that.

At this time I happened to be dating Sherry Smith, although it was something of an arranged relationship. Like most other couples in our eighth-grade class, we were paired by the girls. Several months earlier, Barbara Hill had approached me in the hall.

"Kobe, would you like to date Sherry?"

I didn't hesitate. "Sure, I'd like to date Sherry. Why?"

"She asked me to ask you. Are you going to the party next Friday night at Lynn Ragsdale's house?"

"Yeah, I was planning to."

"Then you'll be Sherry's date," Barbara said and walked away.

Almost every Friday night we would gather at someone's house, usually a girl's house, to listen to music, have something to eat, dance, and then make out until ten or eleven o'clock. If you didn't have a partner, you would try to pair up, even if only for the night, with one of the available girls. If that wasn't successful, it would be an early evening and you headed to Skelton's or Lindale's to get a Coke before going home. Lynn Ragsdale was in the popular group and apparently it was her turn to host the party.

The host girl's parents would greet you at the door and show you to the basement steps. The record player would be spinning 45s of rock-and-roll hits from the radio. The records always belonged to the girls because boys just didn't buy them. The hostess's parents would bring down some food, say hello to everybody, and then adjourn upstairs. The lights would dim and then the dancing would start, which was really no more than two bodies standing toe-to-toe, gripping each other, and rocking back and forth. Fast music wasn't favored; that's not why we were there.

There were usually 16 to 20 boys and girls at these parties and a limited number of sofas and easy chairs. As the dancing progressed, it became important to secure a make-out spot. These were coveted locations and, once occupied, were seldom relinquished. It was all part of the mating ritual: You couldn't appear too aggressive but you didn't want to be left without a place to nest. Timing was very important.

I had dated other girls in the past. In most cases I brought them into the popular group and got them invited to parties they otherwise would not have attended. The opportunity to be paired up with Sherry Smith, though, was big news for me. This was a real step up. Sherry was not only cute but smart, one of the smartest girls in our class. I spent the rest of the day telling all my friends that I was dating Sherry Smith, although I hadn't spoken to her yet.

The make-out sessions gave us boys an opportunity to get some "hand-goodies," also referred to as "copping a feel." I hadn't had much success in this endeavor and I didn't have any illusions of improving my record with Sherry Smith. She wasn't that kind of girl. For me to make the attempt and then have word get around would not be in my best interest. I saw this as an opportunity to secure my position in the popular group.

It turned out that we did officially start dating, and I decided to avoid all locker room talk as long we did. I knew it wouldn't be a long-term relationship and figured my time with Sherry would lead to better things in the future. After all, we're just in eighth grade and had four more years together.

We were still dating a few months later when she was nominated as one of two candidates for vice principal. I did everything I could to campaign for her and started thinking that there might be something to this; maybe it was more than just a temporary arrangement.

As was the normal practice, the cool group met on the front steps of the school before first period, mostly to be seen in our white buck shoes, button-down collars (unbuttoned to indicate we were dating someone and thus not available), and thin white belts with two buckles. Today Bob Evans, Sherry Smith, and Butch Forsyth were missing because, we assumed, they were inside receiving final instructions before taking control of the school. We felt proud to be their friends and knew this would be a special day.

The bell rang and we headed to homeroom. We hadn't been seated more than five minutes when a runner from the front office entered our classroom. "Kobe Grinkmeyer," he said, "is requested to come to the front office."

This was going to be better than I thought! Sherry, Bob, and Butch were summoning me for one heck of a good day.

I gathered my books, headed for the door, and as I left the room, I looked over my shoulder and grinned at my classmates, who I knew were all thinking, "What a lucky guy."

"What's this all about" I asked the runner. "What's going on down there? Were you told to get other people as well?"

"I was just told to come get you. I don't know what's going on."

I entered the front office and was greeted by Butch. "Your mom's on the phone and she says she needs to speak to you immediately." He pointed to a phone on a desk in the corner of the office. I looked around and saw Sherry sitting behind the desk with a questioning look on her face.

I picked up the phone. "Hello, Mom."

I can still remember her words half a century later.

"You tried to kill my baby. Why did you try to kill my baby?"

"What?! I don't know what you're talking about."

"Yes, you do. You tried to kill Stephen last night."

"Mom, I don't know what you mean."

Butch was standing a couple of feet away, Sherry was watching me through the glass in the vice principal's office, and Bob was heading toward me. I was sure they all could see the shock on my face. I certainly didn't want these people to know what my mother was saying so I turned my back to them and faced the wall. I chose my words carefully as I responded to Grace's accusations.

"You left the window in your room open last night so that the cold air would blow on Stephen's head and kill him. Your plan didn't work. Your father will deal with you this evening." Then she hung up.

I put the phone down and continued to face the wall. I didn't want them to see what my face was showing. I had left the window open, that was true. It had been hot last night when I went to bed, so I opened the window to cool to room down and forgot to close it when I got up. My intent was certainly not to kill Stephen. She must know that. Why is she accusing me? What is Dad going to say?

Bob Evans interrupted my racing thoughts. "Kobe? Are you okay?"

I turned around to find Bob and Butch standing in front of me. Bob spoke again.

"Are you sure you're okay? What did your mom want?"

"Nothing. Better get back to class," I replied, moving past them, making sure not to look into the vice principal's office.

Back in class, I returned to my desk and didn't hear a thing around me. All I could hear were Grace's words. "You tried to kill my baby." That's all I heard the rest of the day. I was angry. How could she think that I tried to kill Steve? That is insane.

By ten-thirty I started to doubt myself. Maybe I *am* a bad person. Maybe I *did* try to kill Steve. Could I have done that?

At lunch, I took my food down to the gym and ate alone in the locker room. My study hall was at two o'clock, so I had an uninterrupted hour to think this through. Maybe I did resent the way Grace deserted Butch, Rooney, and me. Maybe I did like it better before Steve joined our family. I would have to watch myself from now on.

I got on the bus after school, dreading my arrival home. I told Butch what had happened. "I told you she was crazy," he said. "I told you."

Although his words were comforting, I didn't think they would go far at the trial I knew would take place that night. Nor would his words have any bearing on my punishment for this heinous act that I allegedly committed against Grace and her son.

I didn't know what to expect. I wasn't accused of talking back. I was being accused of attempted murder! What punishment comes with this crime?

The school bus stopped on the corner of Kirby Avenue and Greencroft Drive. It was just a short walk to the front door, across the dining room, and past the kitchen but Grace wasn't there. Instead I found Wilma, our housekeeper, in the kitchen. Wilma was always gone before we got home from school.

"Your mother took Steve to the doctor this morning and asked me to stay over and fix dinner for you boys and your dad. She didn't seem too happy with you."

"Wilma, she thinks I tried to kill Steve last night," I told her.

"Yes, she told me all about that. Don't pay her no mind. She's just an over-protective mother. You didn't do anything wrong."

Wilma was a Negro lady who had worked for Grace for years before we came along and joined us at Greencroft. She came twice a week to clean and help around the house. Sometimes when Grace and Dad would go away for several days, Wilma would stay with us overnight. Every night she would heat a curling iron on the stove, put something called Royal Crown Gel on her hair, and try to straighten it. At the time I couldn't understand why she would endure such a smelly process to straighten her hair.

"I'm not so sure, Wilma. Maybe I did leave the window open on purpose. I don't know."

"Boy, you're being silly. I've seen you and your brothers around Steve and there is no hate in your heart. You're a good big brother and your mother will get over it. Besides, there's nothing wrong with Steve. She called from the doctor's office and he's just fine. They stopped at Grace's mother's house and will be right home. You go on up to your room and wait for your dad to get home. You and I both know you have a beating coming tonight. Now you go on."

"Steve is okay?" I asked for reassurance.

"He's just fine. Now go on so I can have your father's dinner ready."

I climbed the steps to my room. I figured on a verbal beating from Grace but knew the real punishment would be administered by Dad. He would walk in from work, having spent the day on the highway and meeting with clients selling them furnaces and air conditioners. He would be told by Grace that his second son had tried to kill his fourth son – her baby. He would be asked, "What are you going to do about it?" And everyone knew that whatever the punishment, it would not be sufficient.

I did, however, take some comfort in knowing that my fate would be resolved prior to Dad having dinner. In the past, if there was discipline to be delivered, no one ate until Grace approved of whatever punishment Dad proposed.

Just as Wilma had said, Grace arrived home with Steve. They remained downstairs while I stayed in my room. She didn't want to confront me, and I didn't want to confront her.

Dad came home about five-thirty, and as soon as the door closed, I could hear Grace: "Your son, Kobe, tried to kill my baby last night!"

"What?"

"He opened his window to allow cold air to blow on Steve's head all night and then left the window open in the morning to finish the job, she sobbed, then added, "I took Steve to the doctor this morning and got some medicine to fight a cold or infection."

I lay on my bed, listening their conversation.

"Is Steve okay?"

"He is for now, but what is Kobe going to do next? He tried to kill my baby!"

"Grace, I'm sure Kobe didn't try to kill Steve. It was an accident. I'm sure he never even thought about the cold air blowing on Steve."

"I'm not so sure. I won't give him another chance and moved Steve's bed into our room. What are you going to do about him?"

Dad continued to offer a logical explanation.

"It was an accident, Grace. He didn't mean any harm to Steve." But that wouldn't be the end of it. Grace was sure there was malicious intent and so my actions would need an appropriate response.

After a half hour's discussion and a martini, Dad climbed the steps and entered my room. I sat up on the edge of my bed. He stood over me. "Your mother told me what happened. Did you leave the window open on purpose?"

He didn't ask if I tried to kill Steve because he didn't believe it.

"It was an accident, Dad," I whispered. "I would never try to kill Steve."

"I know," he said, in a low voice. "But I'm going to have to give you a beating, and you'll be grounded for two weeks, and you'll have extra work to do around the house every day when you come home from school for those two weeks and over the weekends. I'll let you know what that is tomorrow morning. Now lay down on the bed and roll over."

I flipped my legs up on the bed. He took off his suit coat, loosened his tie, and took the belt off his pants. He doubled it in his hand so the buckle and the end could be gripped, raised it over his head, and proceeded to give me ten whacks.

Dad left my room and I stayed put. Later, he called me for dinner and I answered that I wasn't hungry. I was actually very hungry but I didn't want to face Grace. Apparently, she didn't want to see me either because there was no objection to my absence. The next two weeks I avoided Grace and stayed away from Steve. I spent a lot of time in my room.

I spent the next two weeks washing windows, pulling weeds and mowing grass. I even did some painting. All these were chores that Butch and I would have done anyway sooner or later.

To say that Grace and I had an adversarial relationship from that point forward would be incorrect. A line drawn had been drawn. I knew where I stood, and I knew how to keep the peace.

# Chapter Twenty
## I Can Be Loved and I Can Give Love

My relationship with Sherry grew stronger through the school year and we became an item, a pair. We were going steady. It felt good to have a girlfriend, a girl who liked me, someone who thought I was special. I couldn't use the word love because I didn't know what it meant. At that stage, our relationship was more about convenience.

The YMCA held teen dances every other Friday night where a disc jockey would play records. I would meet Sherry there and we would dance only with each other. I wasn't into fast dancing but the girls would dance together when the tempo quickened. But when the DJ would play *Smoke Gets in Your Eyes* by the Platters or Paul Anka's *Put Your Head on My Shoulder*, all us boys going steady would grab our girls and hold them tight. We'd barely move our feet.

After the dance, most the steadies would walk to a hamburger joint called Lindale's and get a Coke and something to eat. That is, everyone except Butch and me. Grace and Dad forbid us to walk the streets after dark. It was a big disappointment because the one-mile walk to Lindale's was really about the chance to duck down an alley with your girlfriend and make out.

There was a week when Grace and Dad were out of town and Grandma Grinkmeyer came from Cincinnati to take care of us. Grandma couldn't drive, so we arranged for another parent to pick us up at Lindale's after the dance.

Me and Sherry and Butch and Eileen Daily left the YMCA and headed to Lindale's. It was a warm spring evening and the moon was bright. About halfway there, we took a right turn, went a half a block, and turned into an alley. We stopped at a garage door and I put my arms around Sherry, pulling her close and kissing her. She kissed me back. We pulled each other tighter. I could feel her blooming breasts against my chest, and she pressed her legs tight into mine. We continued to kiss and hold each other tight. In the middle of an extended kiss, I felt her tongue touch my outer lip. I pressed my tongue through my lips and met hers. I could feel the bumps on her tongue. She inhaled heavily and the tips of our tongues danced. I opened my eyes and her eyes were shut; her face lit by the soft glow of the moon. She pulled back, opened her eyes, and gave me the warmest, softest smile I had ever seen. She slowly closed her eyes which I interpreted to mean, "Let's keep going."

I placed my hand in the nape of her neck and kissed her softly, then pressed my tongue to her outer lip. I felt her mouth open and I probed deeper. She ever so slightly pressed her teeth onto my tongue and then opened her mouth wider, pushing her way into my mouth. Our tongues danced in each other's mouths. Sherry pulled back and again we were looking into each other's eyes, trading smiles. Again, she closed her eyes and leaned forward into my awaiting kiss. I felt her tongue dart deep into my mouth, retreat back out, and then return even deeper. A rush went through my body just short of the explosions between my legs I had so come to enjoy. But this was something entirely different. She pulled back, and I knew that Sherry Smith and I had just traveled ground that neither of us had been on before. She closed her eyes and leaned into my shoulder, placing her head next to my neck.

As I held her and attempted to catalog my feelings, I saw something moving toward us and heard the sound of crushing leaves under tires. I focused and saw a car coming down the alley without its lights on. As it neared, I realized it was a police cruiser.

"Sherry, Eileen, run behind the garage and hide. Butch and I will take care of this."

They disappeared just before the policeman turned on his spotlight, illuminating Butch and me. We turned and started to walk down the alley, away from the car. "Just keep walking," Butch said.

"Hold it right there," a strong voice commanded. We stopped and turned.

The officer got out of the car and approached us with a flashlight. "What are the two of you doing here?"

"We were just walking to Lindale's from the YMCA dance," Butch answered.

"By yourselves?"

"Yes, sir," I respectfully offered.

"Come with me and get in the back seat of the car."

We climbed in and he slammed the door behind us. He walked around, got behind the wheel, started the car, turned on the lights, and drove down the alley.

He's taking us in, I thought. He's taking us to jail for making out in the alley. What will Grace and Dad say when they get home?

The car emerged from the alley and turned onto a side street. The officer pulled over next to the curb, put the car in park, turned on the interior lights, and turned around.

"What are your names?"

"Kerry Grinkmeyer, sir"

"Charles Grinkmeyer, sir"

"You brothers?" he said with surprise in his voice.

"Yes, sir," we both answered.

"I'll ask you again. What were the two of you doing in that alley?"

I was about to speak up and tell him there were two girls hiding behind the garage when Butch said, " I had to pee and I didn't think I could make it to Lindale's, sir"

He looked at us from head to toe, looked out the side window towards the alley, and looked back. "You have any ID?"

"Student IDs," we both volunteered.

"Let's see 'em." We both dug out our billfolds and produced Edison Junior High student identification cards.

"You *are* brothers," he sounded surprised. "You know it's against the law to pee in public places, don't you?"

"Yes, sir, but I couldn't hold it, sir," Butch said.

"Well, I'm going to let you off this time, but I've got your names and don't let me catch you two in any dark alleys in the future. You understand?"

"Yes, sir," we said.

"Then get out of here and stay on the street."

"Yes, sir, we will. Thank you, sir."

We climbed out of the police car and walked slowly to the corner. The officer pulled past us, made a left turn, and accelerated down Green Street. Sherry and Eileen appeared from behind a house and ran up to us. Sherry threw her arms around my neck and put her face right up to mine.

"This has been the most exciting night of my life," she told me. She kissed me, pulled back, and still right in my face, said "Tell us everything the policeman said."

We walked the rest of the way to Lindale's under the streetlights, telling our story. Then we spent the rest of the evening sharing and embellishing our adventure. At one point when Butch and Eileen had the stage, Sherry reached over and took my hand. It was as if time stopped, the sound of voices vanished, and the busboys stopped clanging plates and silverware.

Sherry looked at me and I looked at her. My heart went heavy, my breath went short. This was certainly a very exciting night.

"Kobe, do you think the policeman will call your dad?" someone asked. And the moment was broken.

That weekend Sherry was all that I could think about. I decided that this wasn't a relationship for convenience, at least not for me.

On most Mondays, we would pass in the hallway between classes and exchange hellos but I wouldn't see her until after second period. On this particular Monday morning, she was talking to Barbara Hill and Eileen Daily and as I approached, she turned her hand from her side ever so slightly toward me.

I reached out and took it. She continued to talk to the other girls and then looked at me with the same smile I had received Friday night.

"Can you meet me at the ice rink next Saturday afternoon?"

"Sure, which one? But I don't know how to skate."

"Talk to Bob Evans. He knows all about it. See you after school."

Our relationship flourished through ninth grade and into the summer. I learned to skate at the University of Illinois ice rink. We would meet at movies like *Ben-Hur* or *North by Northwest* and sit in the balcony and make out. Butch and Eileen Daily were always with us. The four of us did everything together.

At Saturday night parties, other guys would make futile attempts at "hand goodies" but Sherry and I agreed that making out was as far as we would go. I knew that her mother had talked to her about what was acceptable and what wasn't I didn't want to get on her mom's bad side. She was one of the top students and I was one of the top jocks and everyone liked seeing us together. I knew that Sherry would remain an important part of my life.

One day Eileen told Butch that she was having bad headaches almost every day. Her parents took her to the doctor and he recommended she go to the university for tests. One week later, she had a brain tumor removed. Butch spent a lot of time at her home while she recovered. She returned to school after the Christmas holiday and looked great. She did have a depression on the side of her temple where they had removed some bone, but she was still a pretty girl. Unfortunately, Eileen died a few months later in May, just before summer vacation. Butch went into a shell and didn't come out for months.

As summer neared, Sherry told me that her mother and father wanted me to come to their home for dinner. Her dad, Warren Smith, did something important at the University of Illinois. I had never been invited to dinner at anyone's home and this was my girlfriend's place so of course I said yes.

They lived in a modest home on Avondale Avenue just up from the high school football stadium. Dad dropped me off in front of the house and Sherry met me at the door, brought me in, and introduced me. Sherry had an older brother, Bill, who I could see was not going to make things easy for me. He had been told to be there.

"Kobe, do you remember you and I meeting before?" Mr. Smith asked after I had been there for about fifteen minutes.

"No sir, I don't," I replied, trying to remember where I would have met someone from the university.

"I awarded you your Eagle Badge about three years ago."

"You did?"

"Yes. I remember your mother was pregnant and came up on the stage with you, so you must have a three-year-old brother or sister."

"Yes, I do. I have a brother, Steve, but I'm sorry I don't remember you."

"Well, I can understand why you wouldn't. That was a pretty exciting night for you."

"Yes sir, it was."

"Did you continue in Scouting?"

My confidence was building. "No sir. I turned my attention to running track and playing football." That, I figured, would gain me some points. It didn't.

"Oh, I'm sorry to hear that. We have a very good Explorer program here in Champaign that I'm involved with. Bill here is in it."

The dinner was good and I didn't spill anything. Most importantly, Sherry thought it went well. We made a point to spend time together over the summer and ran around with several other couples that were going steady.

I entered Champaign High School in the fall of 1959 determined to improve my grades, stay out of fights, and become the best person I could be. After all, I was well-liked and had a girlfriend who I thought liked me as much as I liked her. I had made the junior varsity football team and the coaches had asked me to come out for wrestling after football to keep in shape until track. I was connected and there were people who believed in me and had plans for me.

I still remember the games. On the afternoon of October 6, 1959, our junior varsity team played our counterparts at Mattoon High School and we won 21 to 7. I scored one touchdown and ran for 56 yards. I was flying high. The varsity would play Mattoon's varsity that night. Butch and I were going and would meet all our friends and sit in the end zone. Sherry would be there.

"You know the rules, but let me remind you," Grace instructed Butch and me. "You have to be home by 10, not a minute later. Do you understand?"

"But what if the game isn't over by 10?" I asked.

"Didn't you hear me? I said 10, not a minute later."

"But all our friends will be able to stay until the end of the game," I pleaded.

"Your friends don't live in my house, eat my food, or sleep on my sheets. You keep this up and you won't be going tonight or any other night. Do I make myself clear?"

"Yes," I said as we headed out the front door.

It was a twenty-minute walk to the football stadium. "We'll have to leave by 9:30 to get home by 10," Butch said.

"Nobody else is going to be leaving at 9:30. The game won't be over. Let's just stay until the end of the game and take whatever she has to give when we get home."

"Do you ever want to see Sherry again? You know what she's capable of and Dad isn't going to save you."

He was right. "Okay. We'll leave at 9:30 and run part of the way just to be safe. You wearing your watch?"

"Don't I always?"

The sky was clear and a three-quarter moon had risen as it started to turn dark. I have no recollection of how the game went but Sherry was there. At 9:30 we said our good-byes and climbed down the bleachers. We took some ribbing, but Sherry knew the rules that we lived with and accepted it. We circled behind the bleachers toward the back-stadium gate. There, behind the bleachers, we were confronted by eight Negro classmates.

Racial tension had been high at school for the past several weeks due to name-calling and heavy contact on the football practice field. Butch and I had not been involved, so it came as a surprise when one of the students I had classes with struck me in the face with a pair of drumsticks. My nose filled with blood, my eyes went blank, and my knees buckled. Then I was hit in the stomach, dropping me to the ground. I later learned that Butch was facing a similar attack but had been able to stay on his feet. As I lay on my back being kicked by my attackers,

I looked up to the bleachers into the faces of my friends: Terry Fairbanks, Butch Forsyth, Jay Smith, Bob Evans, and others. Not one of them came to our assistance. Not one felt obligated to put their well-being in jeopardy for ours. A police officer saw what was happening and rushed to our assistance. The attackers ran off. The incident lasted less than a minute.

Butch had fared better than me. The drumsticks had opened a cut above and behind my eye, my nose was bleeding, and my ribs ached. The police officer wanted to take me to the team doctor but we convinced him it wasn't necessary. Butch and I gained our composure and rushed home. We ran most of the way because we knew that taking a beating was no excuse for being late. No one was waiting up for us, so we went straight to bed.

The next morning Grace woke me up. "There's a Mr. Smith and his daughter at the door. They want to talk to you. Are you in some kind of trouble?"

"No. Sherry Smith is my girlfriend."

"I know that. Are you in trouble?" she asked again.

"No," I said, climbing out of bed.

"What happened to your face? Have you been fighting again?"

"No. I was sucker-punched," I said as I put on my shoes and walked past her. "I'll tell you later."

"You better not be in some kind of trouble with that girl."

Mr. Smith and Sherry stood in the foyer. "You kids need to talk. I'll wait in the car." Mr. Smith looked at the side of my face. "Are you… okay?"

"Yeah, it looks worse than it feels."

"Let's go for a walk." Sherry suggested.

The three of us headed out the door. Mr. Smith got into his car and watched us head down the driveway, cross over Kirby Avenue, and into the new housing development still under construction.

"Are you sure you're okay?" Sherry asked.

"I am," I said, wanting to take the focus off the black and blue welt on the side of my face and my swollen nose.

"I didn't see what happened, but Bob Evans and Terry Fairbanks told me that a group of boys attacked you and Butch behind the bleachers."

"Yeah, some friends they are," I said with anger and hurt in my voice. "They didn't even come to help,"

"Kobe, it happened so fast. And when they did go down to help, the police wouldn't let anyone behind the bleachers. I know because I was trying to get to you, and when we finally could get back there, you were gone."

"I thought they were just too scared to help us."

We walked a while without speaking. She reached out to my hand and gripped it tight.

"I didn't sleep much last night. I was worried about you."

I was surprised and pleased but didn't know how to respond.

"My mom and I talked about what I was feeling. Kobe, you are very important to me. I enjoy being with you more than anyone else in my life. I think about you every day, most of the day. And when I don't see you on the weekends, I can't wait to get to school so I can see and be with you. You were involved in a car accident and a man got killed. You banged yourself up on your bike and then last night. It just seems that bad things are happening around you, and it worries me."

Again, I didn't know what to say. She squeezed my hand tighter, stopped, and looked at me.

"My mom says that I'm too young to be in love, that I haven't met enough boys and had enough experiences. I don't know, but I do know I want to have you in my life right now and I need to know if you feel the same way about me."

I was speechless. No one had ever said that they needed me, that they thought about me when I wasn't around and wanted to be with me. I searched for what to say. Could I tell her how I really felt and not get hurt? If I did tell her, would she continue to be there for me or would she reject me too?

"Sherry, I don't know what love is. I don't know if I have ever been loved by anyone so I'm not sure what it's supposed to feel like. But you make me feel different then I have ever felt about anyone." I paused. "You make me feel special," I finally blurted out. "So, if this isn't love, I can't imagine what it must feel like. You're very important to me and I want this to go on."

She smiled and squeezed my hand. We turned and walked further away from our house. Neither of us wanted to go back and leave each other.

"Do I need to get you back to your dad?"

He'll be okay. He's got his morning paper. Let's sit down over there. I want to look at that cut."

We walked over to the front step of a new house. She took my chin in her hand and turned my head to the side. With her other hand, she touched the welt next to my eye.

"Ouch."

"Sorry, I didn't mean to hurt you," she apologized, and then tipped my head further to get a better look.

It was a good feeling to have someone taking care of me. It was a feeling I hadn't had for a long time, not since I had pneumonia back on Church Street.

"Sherry, can I ask you a question?"

"Sure"

"Where did you learn to kiss?"

She turned red and looked away.

"I'm sorry I embarrassed you."

"That's alright, it's a fair question."

She turned back and faced me, then dropped her eyes. "My mom reads a lot. She sometimes reads what she calls romance novels. I sneak them from her room and read some of them. That's how some of the characters kiss in her books. Do you want me to stop?"

"Oh, no. You keep reading those novels."

She looked me in the eyes and smiled; she knew what I really meant. We kissed.

"Can I ask *you* a question?" she said.

"Sure"

"You said you don't know if you have ever been loved. Don't you feel that your parents love you? Don't you feel that your mom loved you before she died?"

I paused for a moment, not sure how to respond.

"I really don't know," I finally answered.

# Chapter Twenty-One
## Young Love is Different Than Parental Love

In January of 1960, Champaign, Illinois, just might have been the best place in the world to be a teenager. At least it was for me. Wrapping up my sophomore year, my future seemed clear. I would finish out my high school career with good grades. Coach Mellon felt we could have a shot at the state football championship my senior year and I could get a scholarship to a small state college. He had connections and would help me, he said. I had kept the same girlfriend for the last two years, and we were still going strong. My life was coming together. I had direction and knew where I was going.

My Blue Jay days were behind me. I felt I was finally a Robin. With hard work and any luck, I could become a Cardinal.

Dad usually got home from work a little after five. He'd go upstairs to shower, then he and Grace would have a martini and we would sit down to dinner around 6:15. Dad loved Grace's meatloaf, mashed potatoes and gravy, and corn. We were all at the table sharing our day's activities. There seemed to be a new peace in the house.

"Boys, your father has something to tell you," Grace announced.

We all looked up at him.

"I've been offered a promotion, a larger territory in Indiana," he started. "I have the opportunity to make over $20,000 a year. I've already been to Indianapolis and have spent some time meeting with my new dealers. Mom and I have found a house that is under construction. It will be done in June."

At that moment, my world, and I suspect Butch's world as well, came to a complete stop.

"I've been to North Central High School, a beautiful new school, and I've met with the football coach, Mr. Smith," Dad continued. "He is looking forward to having the two of you on his team."

"Rooney, you'll be going to Saint Michaels Catholic School. I've met with the parish priest and it is a fine school. It'll be a new beginning for you boys. You'll make new friends in a bigger city with more opportunities, better schools, and a great neighborhood."

A new beginning? I was crying inside. I can't let them see me cry, I repeated to myself. I can never let anyone see me cry.

Dad would be spending most of his weeks and some weekends in Indianapolis until June. We'd all join him after we finished our school year here, and then start in Indianapolis in September.

Butch and I had nothing to say so I assumed he shared my feelings. Rooney seemed excited, but he was only nine so everything was exciting to him. Steve was too young to understand. This did mean that Grace would be moving away from her mother and the rest of her family.

"It's a beautiful home with a big yard and four bedrooms. Butch and Kobe, you'll be sharing a room, and Steve and Rooney will be sharing a room. The fourth room will be for Grandma Plotner for when she visits," Grace explained.

The next day I kept hearing Dad's words: "It'll be a new beginning." But I didn't want to start over. I had done that before. I just want to continue my life on the path it was on. That path had been working.

By late afternoon I found myself across Kirby Avenue again, wandering through the construction site. These people will be having new beginnings, I thought. Maybe that's the natural way of life. Maybe it's selfish of me to want to stay in Champaign. I can be a football star at North Central. I'll have plenty of girlfriends. I'll be in the popular group.

I looked out the back window of one of the new houses and onto a corn field. It looks like tall grass planted in perfect rows, I thought. As I crossed what would soon become someone's backyard, I fell into a run. My stomach knotted up and my breath got short but I kept running, deeper and deeper, into the tall grass. I thought of the three-legged grasshopper that tried to pull itself to safety into the tall grass behind grandma's house. I started to sob and fell to my knees. I tipped over onto the ground, drawing my knees up and my arms to my chest. *I don't want to start over. I don't want to start over.*

Hours later I was still lying in the corn. I had fallen asleep and woken up cold. I opened my eyes. It was dark but I felt better. Maybe Butch was right. Maybe grasshoppers can re-grow their legs. I'll survive this new beginning, I vowed. I'll be a football star and I'll meet another girl.

I walked toward Kirby Avenue and our house. A small light burned in the kitchen. They've already eaten dinner, I thought. I'm going to catch hell. I entered the front door. I could hear the TV in the rec room and a dark living room was in front of me.

"Where have you been?" came Grace's voice from the darkness. I could make out her silhouette against the moonlit window. The red amber of her cigarette glowed as she inhaled, then a white cloud of smoke enveloped her. I had seen her like this before when Butch and I didn't make curfew. It never ended well.

~ ~ ~

"What do you mean, you'll be moving?" Sherry asked.

"My dad has been offered a better job. He's already working over there. We'll be joining him in June. They've already bought a new house."

"What about us?"

"I'll be coming back to visit Grace's mother and brother," I said. We'll still see each other." But I knew it would never happen.

We stepped into each other's arms and I felt what I thought was love. I smelled her hair, I touched her hair, I kissed her lips. I closed my eyes and remembered the life she had ignited in me. "Thank you."

"For what?" she asked, looking into my eyes.

"For being you. For sharing yourself with me."

As the school year wrapped up, Sherry and I drifted apart. She never really hooked up with anyone else and neither did I, but it grew less and less important to spend time together. She had, however, given me a new feeling of confidence that I could find someone to have feelings for, someone to love. When our departure for Indianapolis came, I would leave Champaign knowing I would be okay, that starting over for someone like me wouldn't be that hard.

It was to be a false level of confidence, but it did make the transition easier.

~ ~ ~

In the meantime, spring track kept me busy. As a sophomore, I was the fourth fastest on the team and traveled to all the track meets.

"Kobe, I'd like to have a word with you," Coach Hornaday said one day after practice. He worked with the freshman football team and coached the shot put and javelin in track. Over the past two years, he had always encouraged me.

"I understand you'll be leaving Champaign at the end of the school year."

"Yes sir, we're moving to Indianapolis."

"We're going to miss you."

"I'm going to miss Champaign."

"Of all the boys on the team and all that I've ever coached, you've showed more determination and courage than any other. You'll do well in Indianapolis, and you'll be a success at anything you pursue in life. Just keep your can-do attitude." He shook my hand and turned away.

"Thank you, sir." I pushed my chest out and held my head high.

"Oh, Kobe, one more thing."

I turned to look back at him.

**WHO** YOU ARE AND **WHY** YOU ARE YOU

"We all knew that you cut the line at freshman tryouts last year."

~ ~ ~

# Part II

## Discover Your You: What's Your Story?

That's my story. That is who I am and why I am who I am. I share it not for you to know *my* story but to see that by revisiting and understanding your own story, you, too, can be freed from the guilt, insecurity, lack of confidence, and low self-worth you might be carrying and that is holding you back from manifesting your biggest dreams.

"I don't have any of those issues," some of you might be saying.

If that's what is going through your mind right now, if you believe you have truly achieved your full potential, do me a favor and answer these questions:

- Are you happy with your life?
- Are you pursuing your passion or working at "a job"?
- If you had the chance to reinvent yourself, would you? What would that look like?

As I've moved through life, I've come to realize that mine was not a normal childhood, but then what is normal. Some of you may think I had it easy: I always had a meal on the table, a roof over my head, and an older brother I could lean on. Others would say my childhood was filled with drama and that what I experienced wasn't normal.

Whatever your childhood was like, it formed you. It's the foundation that built your character. If you want to find true happiness, I believe it's essential that you revisit those formative years and come to know yourself in a new and deeper way. I have a close friend who spent time with a psychologist while in her early twenties. When she told me that he really helped her, I thought that to seek help like that would be a show of weakness. But now after writing this book at 75 years old, I wonder: "What if I had told this story to a psychologist when I was 30? How would my life have been different?"

Whether you seek such guidance or prefer to go it alone, I think the first step is to revisit your past, those early years, and find those ten days that made you…you. I offer the following steps to help get you started:

**Step #1**: For the next two weeks when you first wake up in the morning, keep a note pad next to your bed and start writing down the 10 to 20 days or events that you feel formed your character.

**Step #2**: At the end of this two-week discovery exercise, share your top days and events with your parents, grandparents, and siblings – anyone who can give you additional pertinent input. Don't allow them to change your list; this is *your* list. You seek their input only to enhance your memory, not to change it, because your character was formed on your memory of events and not on actual facts.

**Step #3**: Start writing and building a narrative – a story – that not only includes the event but also how you feel that event formed who you are today.

**Step #4**: Self-evaluate: In one paragraph, who are you?

**Step #5**: What do you want to change about the current you?

**Step #6**: What are you willing to do to make these changes?

**Step #7**: What is your passion?

# Chapter Twenty-Two
## Are You Willing to Change?

Below is a copy of an email I received this morning while in the process of finalizing this book. LaMarcus is exactly who I'm writing this book for, his letter a confirmation that I'm on the right path and that what I have to share is needed by him and others like him. I wrote him back that I was in my final edit but gave him an exercise and said I'd have the book to him within thirty days.

*Good morning Kerry,*

*I am up late watching YouTube and came across your videos. Listening to your video, I too am searching for myself at this time.*

*I always thought about investing, but never felt that I had the money to do so.*

*After being fired from my past three jobs, I am at the point to where I have to sell my house. I am really trying to find something that I can do and enjoy life while doing it.*

*You seemed really genuine while giving the background of yourself and how you came to be where you are in life and I would love to be mentored by you.*

*I am just looking for keys to be successful in life. I am 40 years old. I am a graduate of University of North Texas and an Army Veteran. I am just reaching out because I really need the help and knowledge so I can be financially successful as well as enjoy life.*

*Thanks for your time and hopefully I will hear back from you. Also, I am willing to work for free as long as you teach me what you know.*

*Thanks,*

*LaMarcus*

The largest obstacle you will have to overcome in order to implement your desired change is you. When I say you, I'm speaking of that unwanted roommate who lives in your head and starts most conversations with "Can't," "Don't," and "That would be a mistake because . . ." Of all the conversations you will have in your life, 90% of them you will have with yourself and most will be negative. So, the first thing you need to do is evict your roommate.

Next, you must decide what you are willing to do to succeed. For example, are you willing to change jobs and start a new career that might require some sort of return to school? Are you willing to sell your home and move into your parent's basement until you can get the education you need? Are you willing to divorce your spouse if he or she will not support you?

I know this all sounds a bit dramatic, but a lot is at stake when you commit to living your dream and being happy. If you have done the work and know who you are and why you are who you are and have discovered your passion, then it's time to pursue it. If you find yourself hesitating, what is in the way? Will you choose to stay on your current path or are you willing to change? It is a conscious decision that only you can make.

Do not respond with "I want to" or "I don't want to." It will have to be, "I'm willing to," followed by specific steps of what you're willing to do to achieve happiness. Your activities define what you are. You are wired to achieve whatever and wherever your actions lead you.

Consider the following statement:

"My goal last year was to earn $100,000 and I only earned $60,000."

You earned $60,000 because you were only willing to do what it took to earn $60,000. Be honest with yourself: Did you relentlessly pursue that $100,000 goal or were there certain things you were not willing to do, such as work more hours, make more phone calls, or expand your contacts. You will know the answer to that.

This is an important step in the process of change. If you aren't willing to do what it takes to go where your passion points you, there's no purpose in going any further. Be honest with yourself or you will waste a lot of time and energy and may even destroy what you have now. Look back at your past attempts at change to discern any patterns. For example:

**My New Year's resolution was to lose 30 pounds.**

Did you lose those pounds? If not, did you do what was needed? Why not? Whose fault was that?

**I need to get out of this relationship.**

Did you? If not, why not? Be honest. There's no one to blame but you.

**I want to get a promotion at work.**

Did you get that promotion? If not, why not? Again, it likely wasn't someone else's fault. What were you not willing to do to get it?

I want to again emphasize the importance of such self-evaluation. If you make a major change to improve your life but fail to meet your goal, the likely reason is that you lack the commitment to do what it takes. This could screw up your life and the lives of others.

So again, we're back to the idea of change. If you continue to do the same things, you'll get the same results. You may have dreams of a brighter future, but you are not your thoughts – you are what you do – so to reach your dreams you must change what you do.

I am not saying that change is easy because it seldom is. It is often fraught with uncertainty. But uncertainty is where new things happen, where opportunity is born. Uncertainty is where you will grow and separate yourself from the competition.

So, get connected with your immediate reality, put aside the negative head speak, and realize that while everything won't happen according to your plan, it's more important to keep moving. Pivot when you must, change your plan, take responsibility for the reality of your situation, and move forward. Do not live in your past; live in your future.

# Chapter Twenty-Three
## Uncertainty Breeds Opportunity

It is human nature to gravitate towards the known, to where you've been before, to where you're comfortable:

- That's why you get up every morning and go to the same job whether you like it or not. It's comfortable, it's certain.
- That's why you stay in the same relationship you've wanted to get out of for the past three years.
- That's why you don't lose the weight; it's easier and more comfortable to just let your waistline continue to grow.

To make a change would take you into uncharted waters where you might make a fool of yourself. At least that's what your roommate keeps telling you. "You're safe here and you want to stay safe."

This attitude permeates all aspects of our lives. We buy the same brand names over and over, go to the same coffee shop, run with the same people. When was the last time you went to a "Meet-Up" where you knew no one? "That wouldn't be safe."

To most people, risk is something to avoid.

How do *you* feel about risk? Does the word bring *fear* into your mind or is it followed by the word *reward*? Risk and reward go hand in hand – the larger the risk, the larger the reward. How do you feel about that statement? How does your roommate feel about risk and reward?

The collective attitude of you and your roommate regarding risk and reward is completely based on experience. If you danced with monsters and goblins in the past and almost got eaten alive, you will probably avoid risk at all costs. On the other hand, if you conquered those monsters and enjoyed the fruits on the other side of the fight, you're probably up for all challenges.

Put simply, this is one of the reasons why the rich get richer and the poor get poorer. It's not because they have more to start with; it's because they're willing to risk what they have to get more.

The age of the Internet has reduced the risk associated with change. You can research your plan and determine your odds of success much easier than you could in the past.

When I decided to commit fully to my YouTube channel, I found plenty of YouTube creators willing to share their path to success as well as their analytics so I could see what it would take and what the potential reward was likely to be. Then I had to make a decision: Was I willing to do what it took to succeed, which would mean making videos and improving my skills? It was a risk but a calculated and educated one, and I determined the risk was worth the potential reward.

I brought a degree of predictability into my new adventure by building an Excel spreadsheet to keep me focused on the prize. This is critical because doubt and disappointment still creep into my mind speak. The spreadsheet refocuses me on the goal and the need to keep deciding: "Am I still willing to do the work?"

Am I certain that I'll hit one million subscribers by September 2021 as my Excel spreadsheet predicts? No! I'm also not certain what other opportunities might emerge between now and then. What I am certain of is that I will find opportunity in that uncertainty. That's where my dreams will be realized. I've abandoned the safety that certainty provides. I will not live in the past. I choose to participate in the future. I also know that I will have to make some tough decisions. Some I'll get right and some I'll get wrong, but the worst thing that can happen is to do nothing at all.

I see myself in a race for those one million subscribers and all other YouTube creators as my competition. I take comfort in knowing that most of them will quit and drop out of the race but it will still come down to me: Am I willing to do what it takes to reach my goal?

If I hit one million subscribers by September 2021, my projections tell me that I'll be making more than Lebron James' $88 million contract. That's a moonshot.

What is *your* moonshot? What are you willing to do? What's keeping you from going for it?

In 1994, a young man of 31 with his 24-year-old wife left their secure New York City jobs in the financial industry and rented a garage in Seattle to build shelves to hold books that he planned to sell over this new form of technology called the Internet. Do you think they went to bed at night with their in-head roommates questioning their thinking? Was there uncertainty? Of course there was. Do you think they had to pivot and change plans, probably more than once? Absolutely.

This guy's name is Jeff Bezos, founder and CEO of Amazon.com. I suggest you read *The Everything Store* by Brad Stone which documents the meteoric rise of this online behemoth. When you need to restore some faith in yourself and your dreams, be sure to read (or re-read) the early chapters.

This is a clip of what Bezos said to the Baccalaureate Class of 2010 at Princeton University. The title of his talk was, "We Are What We Choose."

*"When you are 80 years old, and in a quiet moment of reflection narrating for only yourself the most personal version of your life story, the telling that will be most compact and meaningful will be the series of choices you have made. In the end, we are our choices."*

In leaving their Wall Street jobs, Jeff and Marlene gave up their secure salaries and sizable bonuses. When asked some years later how they came to such a decision, he reflected on that 2010 commencement speech: *"I knew that when I turned 80, I would not regret passing on the bonus, but I would regret not making the choice to fulfill my dream of an everything store."*

# Chapter Twenty-Four
## Convert Your Roommate into Your Biggest Supporter

Change your thoughts and change your life. When you continue to do what you've always done, you are living in the past. You are repeating things that at one time were new and risky but have been turned into a routine. Change your routines, accept uncertainty, be willing to get uncomfortable, and you will get closer and closer to reaching your potential and finding happiness.

What is your relationship to procrastination? Do you tend to delay your to-do list until tomorrow and then the tomorrow after that? Does your mind speak convince you that, "I'm just not up to it today," so instead you surf the Internet or re-check your email? Have you become a clock watcher? Are your relationships a bit rocky? Do you feel you're stuck in a rut?

These are all signals that you need to make changes in your life, if you want to make your life better. You will never get rid of your skeptical roommate, that nagging inner voice that holds you back, but you can change the conversations you have with it. First you will have to overcome those past experiences that have set the tone of your in-head conversations.

You will have to create new experiences that your mind can use as reference points for starting a different conversation, a more life-affirming one.

What separates successful and happy people from unsuccessful and unhappy people is their ability to get past their negative thoughts and focus on positive actions. We all have negative thoughts: I'm not up to this. I'm not worthy. I'm being judged. I don't fit in. I don't belong. I can't do this. This is going to turn out bad. Successful people have found a way to overcome them. And success breeds success, happiness leads to happiness. You get a win, it's easier to get the next one.

To change your path, you will have to take action, you will have to take a first step. That first step is to change the way you look at your life.

So let's start with a question: What is it that you really want? Love, recognition, happiness, a family, to lose weight, a corner office, wealth and fame? Whatever it is, please write it down now:

**I want _____.**

Now let's give it some shape:

**What does_____ look like?**

_____

**What is the first step to achieving _____?**

_____

## WHO YOU ARE AND WHY YOU ARE YOU

Pretty simple, right?

If you're having trouble figuring out this first step, it probably has something to do with educating yourself on *how* to envision and achieve what you want. Fortunately, there are plenty of tools for exploring: A Google search, reading a book, taking a class, going to a conference, seeking advice, to name just a few.

Your goal is to identify your path going forward. The next step is to change your roommate's mind set, which essentially is about changing your subconscious. The simple exercise above won't make every day from here on a great one; you will still have negative, sabotaging thoughts. But once you start seeing progress, you will find yourself in a zone that you don't want to leave because you will have started to discover *you*, and you will like the new you.

You'll become intolerant of those things you used to fall back on: your phone, your email, the guys wanting to talk about the game. That will become nonsense because you now have a mission. You will no longer find short-term happiness in your usual distractions. This new state of commitment will become "the zone," your drug of choice.

You're going to find that your roommate will want to get involved; that's good, invite them in. Find productive time to spend with your roommate, a time without interruption. I have my best collaborative conversations with my roommate in the early morning when I wake up or on a warm afternoon walking in the park. These conversations start with a reflection on a topic that I've studied the day before, for example, we're now deep into COVID-19. Yesterday I read an article on how the Israeli government is planning to open up their economy, allowing people to go back to work based on the type of work they do. Those with the least social contact will go back first, then scaling up in two-week intervals. The last statement in the article was, "None of this will apply to those people with pre-existing health conditions or over the age of 60."

My roommate said, "They're culling the heard, just like your Uncle Wilber did with his cattle."

Do I dare do a video on "Culling the Heard." Will our governments be going into livestock management?

This was a productive boardroom conversation between my roommate and me that gave me something to build on. This is how it goes now: We work as a team; he gives me positive input.

Now that you're getting your roommate on board, find people who think like you. This can be difficult because most of the people in your life right now probably aren't where you are or where you are going; they're back where you used to be, in that negative world you have put behind you.

I have a YouTube channel, "Best of Us", where I share my thoughts and ambitions, and a few like minds have surfaced. I reached out to them and we now schedule regular phone calls which end in a spirit of exhilaration, inspiration and a new level of self-confidence. But first I had to study YouTube and make that first video. Then Monika in Florida responded, and Carlos wrote and asked if he could meet me when I was in San Diego for a Social Media Marketing World Conference.

You see, I'm not on this journey alone, but I started it by myself when I took the first step. I believe I can build a successful YouTube Channel, write and sell books, sell "Best of Us" Investor merchandise, and create courses to teach people what I've learned. I have become my actions, not my thoughts, and this book is one of those actions. My thoughts have become my biggest supporter, they have become my dreams, and my dreams have no limits.

I am what I do.

You are what you do.

I find that I learn best by modeling myself based on other successful people. With that in mind, I share below what I'm doing, how I got there, the thoughts I've had, and the actions I've taken. My hope is that you can find your path in my path.

# Chapter Twenty-Five
## Building My Personal Brand

Most mornings I wake up between 5:30 and 6:00 and I think. I have learned that this is the most productive time of the day for me because I have no distractions. I have not yet powered my cell phone or flipped open my computer to check emails or my YouTube channel results. I simply open my "mind speak" and we discuss the possibilities of the day, such as what I can share with my YouTube followers or how to promote my listings. But I realize these are only thoughts; they won't lead to the results I'm striving to achieve unless I take action.

My ambitions are big: I want to have as many followers on social media as Lebron James and Taylor Swift. I know I have as much to offer as they do but to a different audience. They've been working on building their audience much longer than I have, but with study and by continuing to refine my skills, I can reach comparable levels. I keep my spreadsheet close by where I plug in the growth rates in all the segments of my channel, project when I'll reach my goal of over one million followers, and chart the revenue the channel will generate from my multiple sources of income. On September 25, 2021, I'll have my one million subscribers and be making as much as Lebron.

Will I have to work relentlessly to achieve these numbers? You bet. Will I have to make changes in my plans? Of course. So why am I so confident it will happen?

First, I threw that negative roommate out of my head shortly after educating myself and proving to my satisfaction that what I dream is possible.

How did I educate myself? I found a group of people who were willing to teach me.

Where did I find them? I started at Audible, an audiobook membership club at Amazon. Remember, I'm dyslexic. I don't read books; I listen to books. For $15 a month, I signed up for a program that provided one book a month. I could return it any time and get another. It was there I discovered some fantastic people who wanted to share what they knew by writing books. I tapped into their minds a lot more cheaply than 28-year-old Justin Sun, who last year bid $4,567,888 to have lunch with Warren Buffett (then subsequently canceled his reservation). I can buy Buffett's latest book on Kindle for $9.99.

(I'll share with you the books I've read and continue to reread on my website, www.BestofUsInvestors.com/store. And to see who I follow on YouTube, go to www.YouTube.com/BestofUs/Channels.)

Twenty years ago, to make a career change like you may be considering would have required you to quit your job and probably enroll in a college or university for more education. That is no longer the case; you can easily start your re-training process with books and all the resources now available online.

Now let's look at some possible scenarios that might fit your circumstances and help you identify your path of change.

**Give up "Employee" and Become a "Business Owner"**

If you're a plumber and you want to become a heart surgeon, well, this advice might not hold true. But if you're an automobile salesman and you want to become a financial analyst for Goldman Sachs, go for it. Your first new job may not be with Goldman, but with learning and training and the building of a track record of investment success, Goldman will open its doors to you.

If you're a plumber and you want to own your own plumbing business, very doable as well. For example, educate yourself on running a small business and then find someone who owns a plumbing business and wants to retire. Offer an exit strategy that provides a way to retire and/or includes payments over time for all those years of hard work. There are 79 million Baby Boomers approaching retirement. Eighty percent of small businesses don't have an exit strategy. This could be the dream opportunity you've been looking for.

Each person and situation will have different needs, of course, but my point is this: Where there's a will, there's a way. Or should I say, where there's a *willingness*, there's a way.

**Superstar Careers that Started on Social Media**

This is the age of the artist whether it be a writer, a painter, a singer, or a sculptor. Social media platforms are offering artists unprecedented opportunities to do book deals, cut records, and sell art. Here are just a few of many examples:

- *Fifty Shades of Grey*, an erotic romance novel written by British author **E. L. James** in 2011, was initially self-published as an e-book. It has made a reported $95 million plus millions more for film and serial rights.

- After making a music industry connection at a Holiday Inn party, singer-songwriter **Halsey** got access to a studio to record her first song, "Ghost." She then posted it to her SoundCloud account. An hour later, she logged onto her Twitter account and discovered it was blowing up. According to *Rolling Stone*, the next morning she had multiple record labels begging to sign her.

- **Shawn Mendes** started making six-second videos of cover songs on one of the early video-sharing sites, Vine. Although six seconds is not a long time to show off your talent, Mendes figured out how to make it work for him and his number of followers soon skyrocketed. According to *Billboard*, by the time he had 300,000 followers, multiple record labels including Island Records, Atlantic Records, Sony Records, and Warner Brothers were reaching out to the then 15-year-old.

- One of YouTube's most well-known success stories is that of **Justin Bieber**. In 2007, he began uploading videos of himself covering artists such as Justin Timberlake and Chris Brown. Thanks to a celebrity-boost from Usher and manager Scooter Braun, he was signed to Island Def Jam Music Group. Bieber currently rounds out the top five for most subscribers on YouTube and, beyond his YouTube success, has sold an estimated 140 million albums worldwide

- **Bo Burnham** was 16 years old when he first uploaded a video of himself on YouTube in 2006 singing a song. It went viral and the rest, you could say, is history as he converted that initial breakout into a successful career in comedy, acting, music, poetry, and screenwriting-directing.

- Supermodel **Kate Upton** first garnered national attention thanks to a viral YouTube video of her chair-dancing at a Los Angeles Clippers basketball game which received over three million views . She's been on the cover of *Sports Illustrated* three times and recently married All-Star pitcher Justin Verlander.

- "I can post a painting and it will sell before the paint is dry," boasts Ashley Longshore, who sells her eccentric pop art for upwards of $30,000 straight off of Instagram.

It all comes down to attracting and growing engaged followers. The more popular your account on major social media platforms such as Instagram or YouTube, the more in demand your art, your song, or your comedy will be. Social media is replacing TV as the best way to build a following whatever you do. In the future, everyone will have a personal brand if they want to succeed in their field.

**Right now, I'm looking for an editor for my book. (I guess I found one!)**

If I were a professional editor, I'd have a website highlighting my experience. I'd have a YouTube channel where I explained my process, offered tutorials on writing and publishing, and shared my current projects, thus promoting my clients' work before they were even published. I'd become human rather than an email or phone call. I might even create an Excel spreadsheet to chart my success and project the growth of my business!

# Chapter Twenty-Six
## The Power of Being Relentless

You've committed to change and you've put in writing what you're willing to do to make that change. You've developed a plan of action and a system to map your progress and hold yourself accountable. Now you must become relentless on your quest to achieve your goal.

Look back over your life and identify your greatest successes. Were they easy? Did they happen quickly, or did you have to work long and hard to achieve your goal, to get what you wanted? Were you always comfortable? Did you face setbacks and have to overcome obstacles? Did others ever tell you to give up and move on, to settle for less?

If you stayed the course and achieved your goal, congratulations! You know what it is to be relentless. If you don't know what I'm talking about, you will have to learn a new skill. Most people don't like discomfort, uncertainty, or risk. That's why "unusual" success is so rare. People make a lot of fuss about "overnight success" stories when someone is unexpectedly discovered, but if you dig deeper, you will usually find that years of hard work went into making the overnight moment possible.

A great example of this is the story of J.K. Rowling. Unlike what some might believe, the Harry Potter author's fame didn't come easy. She struggled as an adult – a single mom living on welfare and trying to support her daughter. It took her seven years to write the story of *Harry Potter and the Sorcerer's Stone* and when she finished, all twelve major publishing houses rejected the book. Fortunately, that didn't stop her.

Relentless people have a plan and stick to it despite all the negative noise telling them to give up and settle for something less. The impossible only becomes possible when you decide it's possible. Then you must construct a plan for how to turn the impossible into a reality.

# Chapter Twenty-Seven
## My Plan to Achieve My Goal

Here is my plan for building my YouTube channel, "Best of Us," into a one-million subscriber success story:

YouTube CEO Susan Wojcicki reported that in 2019, there were over 31 million YouTube channels. The number of channels with more than one million subscribers grew by 65% to 16,000 – .0005% of all channels. I know from decades of experience that 90% of those 31 million YouTubers are hobbyists or won't post another video this quarter. That brings my competition down to 3,100,000; of those, I have more world experience that 80% of them or 620,000.

You can see that my challenge is large but through research, I've been able to bring it down to a number I can except. And because of the plan I've built – along with an Excel spreadsheet I can review every day – I can track the progress I'm making and hold myself accountable. I just have to keep doing the work. That includes posting two to three videos a week, selling this book through my YouTube channel, and continuing to build affiliate program sales. I will also update my current book (*How to Supercharge your Real Estate Business*) under the new title of *Building your Personal Brand Using Social Media* and build and publish my video course in which I will teach what I preach.

Understand what I'm doing: I'm taking what I know and love and sharing it around the world. I'm building a loyal audience that I will just keep giving to with no expectation of getting anything in return. And I continue to educate myself to be the best that I can be.

My business plan will generate multiple sources of income based on a business model built around YouTubes analytics which I can transfer to my spreadsheet for tracking my progress on a daily basis. I relentlessly do my part to make the numbers work because my passion is to create, not work. What I'm doing is a pleasure!

And why, again, do I dare to dream of such lofty heights? Because my Excel spreadsheet says it will happen in September 2021; because I have a plan; because I'm working my plan; because I'm continuing to educate myself every day; because I've written this book; and . . . because I'm relentless in pursuit of my passion.

Please focus on that last statement: **"because I'm relentless in pursuit of my passion."**

Commit to your change, decide what you're willing to do to make it happen, build your plan of action, create your spreadsheet, and relentlessly work the plan.

# Chapter Twenty-Eight
## Bring Order to Your Outer World by Bringing Order to Your Inner World

**Why do some people behave badly? For example:**

Harvey Weinstein, Bill Cosby, Bernie Madoff, Roger Ailes, Lance Armstrong, Lisa Lake, Kathy Griffin, Roseanne Barr, Lorie Lockland, Felicity Huffman.

**Why do some people behave honorably? For example:**

Martin Luther King Jr., Bill Gates, The Dalai Lama, Stephen Hawking, Oprah Winfrey, Michelle Obama, Angeline Jolie

Most of these people you know. By most measures, they've made it to the top whatever decisions they've made, whether good or bad – decisions that either helped or hurt others and supported or broke the rules by which most of us live under. Each of their lives could merit its own book or movie or series and, in many cases, already have.

Why do such polarized behaviors exist? I believe that one's behavior is a reflection and a product of something that happened early in their life which laid the foundation for future actions.

By examining such cases of extreme good and bad behaviors of successful people, you can gain insight into how the events in your own early life have and will continue to direct your future behavior.

For example, actresses Lori Loughlin and Felicity Huffman felt they could break the rules and bribe university personnel to get their children into prestigious schools. Did they know it was wrong? I believe they did. I believe that somewhere in their early years, they were taught or learned that to get ahead, you sometimes have to break the rules. They also believe that money has privileges; that's how you get a good table at restaurants and a first-class ticket on an airplane. I'd also be willing to bet that if you could speak with their children, they would see no harm in what their mothers did for them.

On the other side, why are/were Bill Gates, Martin Luther King Jr., and Oprah Winfrey such giving people? Sure, Gates and Winfrey can afford to be giving, but what about Dr. King? If you look deeper, I think you will find the seeds of their generosity in childhood.

I offer all this because I want to stress the importance of knowing who you are and why you are who you are. Once you gain such valuable knowledge, it will be easier to chart your path to happiness and success because your life will be in focus and that focus will give you the power to overcome the obstacles you will undoubtedly face. Instead of distractions or discouragements, you will see those obstacles as challenges you can overcome. They will be much easier to face down than the junior high school bully.

I want to again emphasize the importance of coming to peace with the disapproving roommate in your head. Once you have come to this peace and your mind talk becomes positive, the two of you will work together to plan your future. And trust me when I say that a supportive and approving roommate will be your biggest supporter, your biggest cheerleader, the source of many new ideas.

Having achieved such a partnership with my roommate, each day starts with a new idea. No conflicts, no wasted energy. He is so creative that he gave me the idea for this chapter! He also gave me the idea for two more videos I want to produce for my YouTube channel. And that was all just this morning.

It never used to be this way. In my last years as a financial advisor and the first years of my retirement, my roommate was constantly chiding me about how I got screwed by Ameriprise and how they plotted against me to force me out of the business. He supported his argument by trying to convince me that the same thing happened with my previous employers. It may or may not be true, but either way, he wasn't helping me move forward.

This is Sunday, and my wife Nita and I have a morning routine that takes me up to noon before I can get to my computer.

Today happens to be Super Bowl Sunday. That will give me a three-hour window to write the first draft of this chapter and the scripts for the two videos I have to shoot next week. One of them involves me learning how to shoot a video in front of a green screen and then editing the video over a fixed image of Lebron James and Shaquille O'Neal. But first I have to determine if what I want to do is legal.

I hope you can start to see how the process of learning who I am and why I am who I am led to discovering my passion which became a near full-time commitment. During this time, I have gained an entirely different outlook on my life. My biggest fear is illness and, in particular, dementia. I'm 75 years old and I have another 25 years of work I want to do!

By sharing my journey, I hope you will up the ante on what you're willing to do to make a major positive change in your life. I hope you will deeply explore your early years, find those 10 days and or events that shaped you, then start building your new life based on what you discovered.

# Chapter Twenty-Nine
## What's Next?

Let's assume you are in your mid-thirties and married with two children. You are buying a home and have a car payment. I hope you have life insurance on you and your spouse and you're contributing to a retirement program. Remember, I'm a retired financial advisor!

This describes me in 1978 when I was 34 years old. I was working for Polaroid in Minneapolis traveling back and forth between Minnesota, North Dakota, South Dakota, and Western Wisconsin. I didn't enjoy my work. I originally took the job because I was fascinated with the photography industry but soon learned that my mission was to sell dealers on advertising Polaroid cameras and push inventory out the door.

Why didn't I leave this well-paying job with a national company? I wanted to be happy and fulfilled but I didn't know who I was or how I became who I was. I didn't know my passion because I never took the time to do any self-examination. If I had looked closer, I would have realized that in my spare time, I was painting the pictures to hang on the walls of the early American home we had built. I would have realized I was a right-brained person who enjoyed creating things. I didn't have the option to explore my interests on the

Internet and reeducate myself. I didn't have Audible or YouTube. If I had, I believe I would have become a videographer and made documentaries.

Although Ken Burns is nine years younger than me, he graduated from Hampshire College in Amherst, Massachusetts, in 1975 with a degree in film studies so the education *was* available. I've checked the offerings at the University of Minnesota, and they do have degrees in cinema and independent film making. What I don't know is whether they had those studies back in 1978.

Not knowing all this, did I leave Polaroid and change my life path? I didn't. Would I have made the career change knowing what I know now? Would my wife, Nita, have supported my decision? Would I have taken the risk?

As for Nita, yes, she would have supported me. I know this because we've been together 53 years and she has always been there for me. As for me, yes, I have no doubt. I would have changed my career. And after reading my life story, you should have no doubt. I would have seen it as a challenge; it would have activated the right side of my brain; I would have been consumed by the possibilities.

What about the risk? Well, we wouldn't have been able to pay our bills and we might have had to sell our home. Been there, done that, and we survived. My attitude has always been, "It's only money. I can always make more."

But that's me. What about you?

I'll go back to Jeff Bezos' statement: *"I knew that when I turned 80, I would not regret passing on the bonus, but I would regret not making the choice to fulfill my dream of an everything store."*

I don't know you but I do know that at some point you will die. When that day comes and you evaluate your life, what are you going to regret?

I can understand if, like the generations that proceeded us, you are happy to have a job and a roof over your head and food on the table. But today you can become anything you want. Maybe not an All Star basketball player but you have unique, God-given abilities that await your attention, that are ready to take you where you *really* want to go, even if you aren't quite sure where that is yet.

# Chapter Thirty
## Create a Flexible Plan

Your plan for your change will most likely involve other people and organizations that you have no control over so be cautious of setting your expectations *too* high. Yes, I have a spreadsheet that serves as my plan for achieving what are clearly very ambitious goals. But I know I don't have control over YouTube's algorithms or a lock on my audience likes and dislikes.

If my channel doesn't grow at the rate I planned for but does keep growing, I must accept that growth and adjust my actions and my plan accordingly. I'm covering new ground and can't allow expectations to derail me. To do otherwise will foster disappointment, resentment, and anger, and nothing good can result from allowing these feelings into my head. It would start to re-empower the bad roommate.

Expectations are different than goals. The path from desire to achievement doesn't usually follow a straight line and flexibility is critical. Whatever you pursue, whether it be a relationship or a new career, you assume you'll succeed but there will be unspoken expectations. They are rooted in those past experiences and relationships and were either met or weren't. Back then when you started a project, you had unspoken expectations of success but success didn't always follow. If you relied on others, for example, they may not have even known of your ambitions. Often there were forces beyond your control. Maybe unconsciously you sabotaged yourself. Whatever the reasons, they sowed the seeds of many of the difficulties you deal with today.

Let's try an experiment. Look at a part of your life that isn't going as you thought it would – it might be your marriage or your job – and write down what you expected to happen and what actually happened. Put them side by side: how you thought it would go, how it actually went, and how you feel about it. The gap between the two represents your pain. Does looking at it this way make you feel any better? Probably not, though the exercise may be revealing. If you concentrate only on the pain, you can't move forward, you can't take corrective action. Accept reality as it is – you are powerless to change it. But you *can* affect what happens next.

Live in the moment, live in reality, and pivot if you must. For me, I enter new numbers into my spreadsheet, determine how best to respond, and move on. This probably pushes the achievement of my goal further out, but the goal remains in sight.

You can't anticipate everything in your plan; just be prepared for some disappointments and know that you have the power to adjust. Expect nothing and accept everything. Love the life you have, not the one you expect to have.

# Chapter Thirty-One
## Commit to Change

If you want the life you only dream about, positive thinking alone won't get the job done. You're going to have to change. It takes positive actions to turn dreams into reality.

I'm confident that this isn't the first book you've read on personal development, but here you are, reading another one. What is holding you back from achieving your potential? I think it's you, the you who lives in your head, your roommate. That roommate is a reflection of all your fears; it's rooted in your past. You need to go back and face those fears straight on, then go back further and find the origins of those fears and come to peace with them. Then you will find the new you to build upon, a you that will stand on a clear understanding of who you are and why you are who you are, with no apologies and with courage to create a new life.

I have found that stating your commitment out loud to someone other than yourself can light a match under your passion. So here's what I want you to do: Go to my website, www.BestofUsInvestors/Commitment, and enter your commitment to change. Tell me the change you are going to make in your life and what you will do next to get there. Then add a reminder to your calendar to come back to the site each month for six months and update your commitment with your progress. Come back as often as you wish after that to update your progress. By doing this, you'll be holding yourself accountable as well as serving as inspiration for others.

I know what you're probably saying right now: "I'll do it later. Now isn't the right time." That would be a good example of procrastinating! And procrastination is not our friend.

The last thing I want is for you to be lying on your death bed and saying to yourself, "If I'd only had the courage to report to Kerry, my life might have been so much better."

You need to act. To change your inner world, you need to act in your outer world. I'm willing to commit to you. Are you willing to commit to me?

My website address is www.BestofUsInvestors/Commitment.

It's my hope that this will become a community of people who can work together and help each other and turn to each other in times of need.

I know how you might be feeling: This guy is calling me out! When was the last time you were called out? How did you react? What were the consequences of your actions or inaction?

You may have bought this book hoping that I had a magic formula. It's not magic, but it is simple:

1. Discover who you are and why you are who you are.
2. Discover your passion and use your passion to change your life.
3. Determine what you are willing to do to achieve your dream.
4. Embrace the uncertainty you are about to take on to achieve your dream.
5. Convert your roommate to your biggest supporter.
6. Relentlessly work your plan to achieve your dream.
7. Bring order to your internal world.
8. Manage your expectations.
9. Go to my website and make your commitment.

The ball's in your court. What are you going to do?

**My name is Kerry. My website is:**

**www.BestofUsInvestors.com/Commitment.**

# Epilogue

There is one more day in my life that I need to share with you:

**December 26, 2014.**

Shannon Marie was born on May 13, 1973.

I drove to the hospital the next morning. Stevie Wonder was singing "You Are the Sunshine of My Life" on the radio. Shannon was a second child, so her life and destiny would be shaped by her mother, father, older brother, and her will. She was a small girl trying to keep up with her older brother (of four years) who loved her very much. He swam on the swim team, so she swam on the swim team; he played Little League baseball, so she played baseball; he played soccer, so she played soccer. It was here that someone other than her family took notice: her coach. Although she was small, she intimidated the other boys and girls on her team and other teams with her skills and became a star. She gained self-confidence and started to form her own identity.

FIND HAPPINESS BY DISCOVERING

At 13, she asked her mom if she would drive her down to the courthouse.

"Why, what do you need to do at the courthouse?"

"I want to change my name."

"Change your name to what?"

"Shannon-Marie Katherine Grinkmeyer."

"Why?"

"You didn't name me after Dad's' mother; I am her reincarnation."

My mother died at age 30, when I was 8 years old, of breast cancer.

The next week, Shannon Marie became Shannon-Marie Katherine.

**July 16, 1988**: Cross-country summer camp at Oak Mountain State Park. Shannon collapsed while running, pain shooting through her foot up into her leg. She was a mile from the cabins in the depths of the woods and she was unable to move it, the pain too severe for her to walk back to camp. Her brother was told of the situation and he ran into the woods to help her. Thirty minutes later, he jogged into camp with Shannon on his back riding piggyback. Little did we know that this wasn't the first time this had happened. It had happened several times over the years but never this bad.

At the encouragement of her coach, she continued to try to run but the pain persisted and grew in intensity. Over the next four years, she visited three doctors who placed arch supports in her shoes and put her into a large plastic boot, but the pain continued. In her effort to relieve the pressure on her left arch, she curled her toes and transferred all her weight to her right foot.

Shannon went north to college on a photojournalism scholarship, 800 miles from home, with new doctors and more medication. She came home the winter of 1991 for a surgery to fix chronic planter fasciitis – what she had been diagnosed with. The surgery alleviated some of the pain for six months, but then it intensified. She graduated in 1992, dealing with the pain the only way she knew how: with medication, a cane, and more doctors.

She had developed hammer toes. One of the doctors cut the tendons in the toes and inserted steel pins into each toe to force them into a normal position. The pain continued and the pain medication strengthened.

Now working in Atlanta, her new doctor told her there was no reason for the pain. He explained that it was all in her head, that she had conditioned herself over the past nine years to expect pain and that her mind was sending signals of what she had grown to expect. He prescribed an electrical shock box attached to her waist that would deliver a painful charge into her back each time her foot hurt as a way to recondition her brain. She tore up the prescription.

Shannon was married on September 30, 2000, to Justin Hamer; that day she and I danced to Stevie Wonder singing *You Are the Sunshine of My Life*. Several months later, she confided in her mother; I will never have children because I am too unstable to care for a baby.

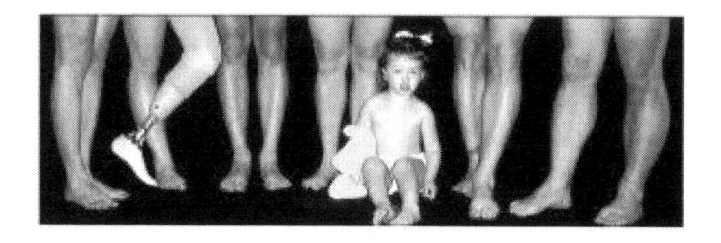

Our 2002 New Year's resolution was to get our daughter's foot fixed. We took her to the Health South Sports Medicine Clinic in Birmingham in late February. They took X-rays and told her to get an MRI. Days later we were told that Shannon had a tumor in her foot that had been there for over 12 years. The tumor had grown up and over her toes, had penetrated the bones in her foot, and was about to penetrate the skin on the top of her foot. "We'll have to take a biopsy to determine if its cancerous," he informed us.

On May 14, 2002, one day after Shannon's 29th birthday, Dr. Kenneth Jaffey offered Shannon a life-or-limb decision.

"It's cancerous. If you leave it, the cancer will spread through your skeletal system and you will die. Or, we can amputate your foot and hopefully we will have gotten all the cancer before it has traveled up your leg."

As Shannon's father, I felt helpless.

"Why didn't I find this doctor ten years ago so my daughter could keep her foot?" I railed. "Why didn't this happen to me?

I've lived my life, I could endure this better than her. What am I supposed to do now?"

Shannon, her husband, Justin, and her mother met with Dr. Monson of Crawford Long at Emory Clinic in Atlanta and the date was set; her foot would be amputated at mid-calf on June 12, 2002.

I had failed my daughter. Why did I allow this to happen?

The next morning as I got ready for work, I had the "Today Show" on. Katie Couric was interviewing Bob Kerrey, former senator from Nebraska. Her final question to him was, "Senator Kerrey, I understand you lost your leg in the Vietnam War. How did that change your life?"

Kerrey explained that coming back from Vietnam without his left leg was the most important event in his life; it had led him into public service. "I know that if I hadn't lost my leg, I would not have achieved what I have."

I decided that I had to get Senator Kerrey to talk to Shannon. I didn't know what to say to her but Bob Kerry would. That day I found him on the internet. He was the president of New School University in New York City. I sent him an e-mail and told him about Shannon. The next Saturday, he called Shannon and talked to her for an hour about the rest of her life.

Shannon had the operation on June 12, 2002. Over the next several months, she was fitted for a prosthetic and started rehabilitation. On December 22, 2002, she fell and shattered her left knee and femur and was rushed to the closest hospital. Justin called and told us that the attending doctor suggested amputating her leg above the knee.

"You tell them to tape her up and get her home. We're taking her to Dr. Munson."

Shannon went to see Dr. Monson on December 23, 2002.

"I don't fix knees, I replace them," he said. "But I know someone who can do it."

On December 26, 2002, surgery was performed on her leg by one of Atlanta's best orthopedic surgeons, Mary Jo Albert. She was given a 40% chance of full recovery. Nine months later, the screws, pins, and hinges were removed and Shannon resumed her rehab.

On May 24, 2005, Justin and Shannon-Marie Katherine Grinkmeyer-Hamer gave birth to Aidan Alistair Hamer.

Shannon lived cancer-free until June 2007 when her five-year check-up found a small tumor on her left lung; she was scheduled for surgery to remove it. I was shocked to find that they had opened her up from under her breast to her shoulder blade, but elated to learn that the surgery was successful and the prognosis good.

Shannon became a successful financial advisor with Ameriprise in Atlanta. She focused her practice on helping young families plan for their financial goals while protecting themselves from the traps of an unexpected illness, having dealt with her own inability to purchase life and disability insurance.

In 2011, another tumor appeared in her left lung and again she underwent painful surgery. She was clean for two years when in 2013, a CT-scan found a tumor the size of a golf ball between her heart and larynx; two weeks later, it was the size of an orange and she was rushed into a program of massive chemotherapy, radiation, and surgery.

In September 2014 the cancer returned and now there were multiple tumors. She was admitted into a clinical trial for a new form of chemo, only to be withdrawn after two months because it wasn't effective. She was then put into another program which required her to be in the hospital for seven days of chemo with one month off for seven sessions over a seven-month period.

In October 2014, Shannon, Alan Vickness, and I participated in "24 Hours of Booty" (a 24-hour bike ride to raise money for cancer research), and Shannon was named "Rookie of the Year." The highest fundraiser was awarded a new Pinarello bike. Seeing this, Shannon declared, "I'm going to win that bike next year." That wouldn't happen, but Aidan, her son, won the bike in 2015.

On December 22, 2014, my wife, Nita, and I were in Atlanta to celebrate Christmas. That morning, Shannon became incoherent; her temperature shot up to 102 °F and she passed out. Nita called 911 and we took our daughter to the emergency room. If this had been any other Monday, Justin and Aidan would have already left for work and school and our daughter would have died alone on the sofa in their family room.

I watched my daughter take her last breath four days later.

For the previous 12 years, Shannon had courageously fought her war against cancer. She won some battles, but the war wouldn't end. During that time, she had gathered an army of friends who provided support and logistics for her and her family. For six years, her growing army gathered every Christmas Eve at her home to celebrate another year's fight, to celebrate her victories. 2014 was to be their last.

Shannon Marie-Katherine died on December 26, 2014; her army gathered on December 31, 2014, to celebrate her life.

**THE END**

Printed in Great Britain
by Amazon